MIND OVER MONEY

Harness The Power Of Your Thoughts To Achieve Wealth And Financial Security

Philip A. Board
MSFS. CFS.

Dedication

To my extraordinary wife, Patricia, whose unwavering love and partnership have been my greatest wealth—and to our two precious daughters, who remind me every day that true security comes from the joy we build together.

You are the heartbeat of this journey, inspiring me to turn lessons in finance into a legacy of abundance for our family and beyond.

With endless gratitude, Philip

Contents

Author's Note

Dear Reader,

As I sit down to share this book with you, I'm reminded of a simple truth that's guided my career for over three decades: money isn't just about spreadsheets and strategies—it's about the stories we tell ourselves, the fears we conquer, and the dreams we dare to chase. When I founded 1on1 Financial back in the early days, inspired by the no-nonsense wisdom of my father, I set out to create more than a business. I wanted a space where people could receive the kind of personalized guidance that changes lives—not just portfolios. Today, as President and CEO, I've had the privilege of walking alongside countless individuals through their financial highs and lows, witnessing firsthand how a shift in mindset can unlock doors to stability, growth, and even legacy-building.

This book is born from those conversations, those "aha" moments in my office, and yes, a few humbling mistakes of my own along the way. It's my way of paying forward the lessons I've learned—from dialing for dollars in my twenties to training advisors nationwide on blending technology with heartfelt service. But I couldn't have reached this point without the incredible team at 1on1 Financial, whose dedication turns complex plans into simple peace of mind. A special acknowledgment goes to my invaluable colleague, Isahi "Mia" Medina—From data entry to now Chief Operating Officer, and Financial Planner. With over 21 years in the industry and her passion for seamless client experiences, Mia has been the operational wizard behind our growth, ensuring every detail aligns with our mission. Her resilience, inspired by her family's journey. Mia, your collaboration has been a game-changer—thank you for helping me build not just a firm, but a family of supporters.

Whether you're just emerging from survival mode or ready to step into builder status, I hope these pages spark the mindset shift you've been seeking. Let's turn thoughts into wealth, one empowering step at a time.

Warmly, Philip A. Board, MSFS, CFS

Chapter One: My Journey Begins

When I first started in finance, I thought it was all about numbers. If you could analyze the right data, track market trends, and memorize investment strategies, you'd be set. But I quickly realized that money is more about mindset than mathematics. The numbers matter, but the way people think about money matters more.

Looking back, I never set out to become a financial advisor. Like most people in their early twenties, I was just trying to figure out how to make a decent living. But one thing was clear—I wanted to make money. A lot of it. And if we are being completely honest, I wanted a Ferrari.

This was the late 1980s, and I had just seen Wall Street. You know, the original one, with Michael Douglas as Gordon Gekko, delivering his iconic "greed is good" speech. I thought to myself, That's the life. That's the job. That's what I want to do. Fast cars, high-rise offices, tailored suits—what could be better? So when a friend of my dad told me that if I could pass my Series 7 exam, he had a job for me, I jumped on the opportunity.

What he didn't mention was that the "job" was essentially a desk, a phone, and a phone book. No salary. No leads. Just me, a list of numbers, and the hope that a stranger on the other end would trust a 20-something kid with their life savings. That's what "dialing for dollars" meant. It was a numbers game, but not in the way people think. It wasn't about understanding stock charts or predicting market movements—it was about who would pick up, who wouldn't hang up immediately, and who might actually say yes.

I was terrible at first. Absolutely terrible. I must have been hung up on a thousand times before I landed my first real client. I remember staring at the phone, questioning every life decision that had led me to that moment. But I kept dialing. Because that's what you did. You put in the hours, took the rejections, and hoped that persistence would eventually pay off.

And slowly, it did.

I started to notice patterns. The people who did invest weren't necessarily the ones with the highest incomes. They were the ones with the right mindset. Some clients earned six figures but were always broke. Others made a fraction of that and were on their way to building real wealth. That's when it hit me—success wasn't just about money. It was about how people thought about money. Their habits, their beliefs, their discipline. The difference between the ones who got ahead and the ones who stayed stuck wasn't just their bank balance. It was their mindset.

The Ferrari vs. Reality

Now, about that Ferrari.

I never got it. Life had other plans. A wife, a family, a mortgage—turns out, those things are expensive. Instead of a bright red Italian sports car, I ended up with something more practical: an SUV that could fit car seats but still had a ridiculous amount of horsepower.

And honestly? I wouldn't trade it. That shift—from chasing flashy wealth to building something sustainable—is the exact thing I want to help others understand.

I have seen too many people sabotage their own financial future because they are stuck in the wrong mindset. Some people never get past survival mode. Others finally make good money, but instead of saving, they jump straight into spending. They think earning more will solve their problems, but it never does—not unless they change how they think about money in the first place.

Therefore, this book isn't just about finance. It's about mindset shifts. It's about moving from one stage of financial thinking to the next, recognizing where you are, and taking control of where you are going.

I have spent years helping people with their money. I have also seen all the mistakes—some of which I have made myself. But what I have learned is that finance doesn't have to be boring or intimidating. If we can laugh at our own bad money habits and recognize where we are going wrong, we can actually change them.

So, I decided to write a book that balances both serious financial strategies with a little bit of humor. Because let's face it—most people don't want to read a dry, textbook-style finance book. They want something practical, something relatable, and maybe even something that makes them chuckle along the way.

This is that book.

If you have ever wondered why you handle money the way you do, or how to finally break free from financial stress, you are in the right place. I cannot promise you that after reading this book, you will get rich overnight. But what I guarantee you is that you will understand how your mindset shapes your financial future—and how you can change it for the better.

One of the biggest lessons I have learned in my career is that people don't struggle with money because they don't earn enough. They struggle because they don't understand how to manage what they earn. This is why some people making $40,000 a year are better off financially than people making $250,000. The income doesn't dictate the outcome. The mindset does.

I have seen people sabotage their financial futures over and over again. They get a big raise, and instead of using it wisely, they upgrade their car, buy a bigger house, or splurge on expensive vacations. They confuse having money with keeping money.

Then there are the people who are afraid of money. They grew up hearing things like "money is the root of all evil" or "rich people are greedy," so even when they do start making good money, they feel guilty about it. They spend it just to get rid of it, or they self-sabotage because they believe wealth is somehow immoral.

And finally, there are the people who understand money for what it is: a tool. These are the ones who build lasting wealth, not because they were born rich, but because they learned how to think about money in a way that served them instead of hurting them.

That's what this book is about—helping you get there. Helping you shift your money mindset so that whatever financial goals you have, you actually get to achieve them.

No fluff. No nonsense. Just the truth about money and how to finally take control of it.

Let's get started.

Chapter Two: The Five Money Mindsets

The Path to Financial Growth

Money is more than just numbers in a bank account; it embodies our habits, fears, beliefs, and aspirations. Throughout my journey, I've identified five distinct money mindsets that influence how individuals manage their finances: Survivor, Spender, Saver, Grower, and Builder. Each mindset represents a stage in an evolving financial journey, and understanding where you currently stand is the first step toward transformation.

I've encountered individuals at every stage—some caught in cycles of debt, others hesitant to take risks, and a few who have mastered the art of building lasting wealth. Their struggles and triumphs have deepened my understanding of what it truly takes to transition from financial instability to financial freedom.

This book goes beyond mere budgeting tips or investment strategies; it focuses on mindset. Your thoughts and behaviors regarding money significantly influence your financial outcomes, often more than your income level alone. Some individuals earn six figures yet remain financially strained, while others with modest incomes manage to build wealth over time. The key difference lies in their mindset—how they think about money, manage it, and leverage it to create opportunities.

Why is this distinction important? Many people are unaware that they are trapped in a mindset that hinders their progress. A Survivor believes they will always struggle. A Spender justifies every purchase. A Saver hoards money out of fear. A Grower learns to make money work for them. A Builder establishes financial systems that generate wealth for generations.

I have dedicated my career to helping individuals shift their financial perspectives. There is a unique satisfaction in guiding someone from one stage to the next—watching them evolve from merely surviving to truly thriving. This book aims to help you recognize your current mindset, understand its limitations, and take actionable steps to move forward.

Whether you're starting from scratch or already making strides toward financial freedom, this journey is about progress, not perfection. Your financial mindset is not fixed; it can be transformed. Once that shift occurs, everything else will follow.

1. The Survivor Mindset: Living in Constant Uncertainty

The Survivor mindset is characterized by financial instability and an ongoing struggle to stay afloat. Individuals in this stage often live paycheck to paycheck, finding it challenging to cover basic necessities without resorting to borrowing or sacrificing other essentials. Every unexpected expense—a car repair, a medical bill, or even an increase in rent—feels like a crisis.

The Daily Struggles of a Survivor

People with a Survivor mindset typically face several challenges, including:

- **High Debt and Financial Stress:** Relying on credit cards, payday loans, or borrowing from friends and family becomes the norm.
- **No Emergency Fund:** Even minor setbacks can derail their entire financial situation.
- **Reliance on Credit for Basic Needs:** Instead of using credit strategically, they depend on it for survival, perpetuating a cycle of debt.
- **Lack of Financial Literacy:** Many Survivors lack the knowledge or guidance necessary to change their circumstances.

I have encountered numerous individuals trapped in this phase, each facing their own struggles and unique challenges. One story that stands out is that of a single mother who worked multiple jobs just to keep a roof over her head. Every dollar she earned was already accounted for before it even reached her bank account—rent, utilities, groceries, and minimum debt payments left no room for savings. Despite her relentless efforts, she felt as if she were constantly drowning.

Her breakthrough moment came when she realized that merely surviving wasn't enough; she needed to take control of her finances instead of allowing them to control her. She began tracking her spending, prioritizing essential expenses, and gradually building an emergency fund, even if it was just $20 at a time.

Shifting from Survival Mode to Financial Awareness

Breaking free from the Survivor mindset starts with awareness. It involves recognizing unhealthy financial habits and taking small, intentional steps toward stability. Some key actions include:

- **Tracking Expenses:** Understanding where your money is going is crucial.
- **Building a Small Emergency Fund:** Even saving a few hundred dollars can prevent reliance on credit for unexpected expenses.
- **Reducing Debt:** Focus on paying off high-interest debts first.
- **Shifting from Reactive to Proactive Financial Mindset:** Transitioning from just getting by to planning for the future.

The Survivor mindset can be one of the hardest to escape, as it often feels like there is no room for change. However, with the right mindset shift, even the smallest actions can lead to financial relief and, ultimately, stability.

2. The Spender Mindset: Trapped in the Cycle of Instant Gratification

The Spender mindset is characterized by a strong emphasis on immediate desires rather than long-term financial well-being. Unlike

Survivors, Spenders typically have a steady income, but their money often disappears as quickly as it arrives. By prioritizing wants over needs, they struggle with impulse control and frequently avoid financial planning. While they may not experience the same level of desperation as Survivors, they remain financially vulnerable due to poor money management.

The Emotional Drivers Behind Overspending

Spending habits are not merely about numbers; they are deeply rooted in emotions. Several key factors contribute to this mindset:

- **Lifestyle Inflation:** As income increases, so do expenses. Instead of saving or investing, a higher salary often leads to a bigger house, a nicer car, or more luxury purchases.
- **Societal Pressures:** Social media, advertising, and cultural expectations create a constant push to keep up with trends, leading many to spend beyond their means.
- **Emotional Spending:** For some, shopping becomes a way to relieve stress, boost confidence, or cope with feelings of boredom, loneliness, or anxiety.
- **The Need for Validation:** Many Spenders tie their self-worth to material possessions, believing that status symbols will earn them respect and admiration.

Caught in the Cycle: A Real-Life Story

One of the most memorable Spenders I've encountered was a young professional earning a six-figure salary yet living paycheck to paycheck. Every time they received a paycheck, it was immediately spent on designer clothes, luxury vacations, and nights out. They justified these expenses by saying, "I work hard; I deserve to enjoy my money."

At first glance, their lifestyle seemed glamorous, but beneath the surface, they were drowning in credit card debt. Despite their high income, they had no savings, no investments, and no financial security. A sudden job loss became their wake-up call—without a safety net, they faced eviction and had to borrow money just to survive.

The Turning Point: Recognizing Spending Habits and Learning Financial Discipline

Breaking free from the Spender mindset requires self-awareness and discipline. Some effective strategies for overcoming this cycle include:

- **Tracking Spending Habits:** Understanding where your money goes is the first step to gaining control over it.
- **Setting Financial Priorities:** Differentiating between needs and wants helps in making smarter financial choices.
- **Creating a Budget with Limits on Discretionary Spending:** Allocating a specific amount for non-essential purchases can prevent overspending.
- **Delaying Gratification:** Implementing a "wait 24 hours" rule before making unnecessary purchases can help curb impulse buying.
- **Building an Emergency Fund:** Having savings creates financial security and reduces the need for reckless spending.

The Spender mindset isn't about deprivation; it's about finding balance. Learning to enjoy money responsibly, without allowing spending to control you, is essential for progressing on your financial journey.

3. The Saver Mindset: Security Over Growth

The Saver mindset represents a significant advancement from the Spender mentality. Savers are disciplined with their finances, prioritizing financial security and typically avoiding unnecessary expenses. They focus on saving rather than spending, often stashing money in savings accounts and steering clear of debt at all costs. While this mindset provides stability and a sense of control, it also has its limitations—saving alone is insufficient for building long-term wealth.

Characteristics of a Saver

Savers tend to exhibit several key traits:

- **Living Below Their Means:** They avoid frivolous spending and actively seek out the best deals.
- **Prioritizing Financial Security:** Their primary goal is to ensure they never fall into financial hardship.
- **Fearing Financial Risk:** They prefer to keep their money in low-yield savings accounts rather than investing it.
- **Avoiding Debt:** Even when it comes to taking on smart debt, such as a mortgage or business loan, they hesitate.

While these characteristics protect them from financial instability, they can also hinder financial growth. Savers often overlook the fact that simply saving money won't generate wealth—investing and growing their money is essential for achieving true financial freedom.

The Benefits and Limitations of the Saver Mindset

Benefits:

- Financial discipline and stability
- Freedom from unnecessary debt
- Strong emergency funds and peace of mind

Limitations:

- Fear of investing leads to missed opportunities
- Savings lose value over time due to inflation
- Hesitation to take calculated risks prevents financial independence

Overcoming the Fear of Investing

I once worked with a client who had been diligently saving for over a decade. They had accumulated a significant amount of savings but were reluctant to invest, fearing the loss of their hard-earned money. Each time they considered investing in stocks, real estate, or even a business, anxiety held them back.

Despite their financial discipline, they were unknowingly losing money due to inflation. Their savings were growing at a sluggish pace in a low-interest account, while the cost of living continued to rise.

The turning point came when I helped them understand the concept of calculated investing—the idea that risk can be managed through knowledge and strategy. They began small, investing in diversified index funds and gradually building their confidence. Over time, they witnessed their money working for them instead of sitting stagnant.

Transitioning from a Saver to a Grower: The Shift from Security to Growth

Moving beyond the Saver mindset requires a mental shift from focusing solely on security to embracing smart financial growth. Key steps in this transition include:

- **Understanding Inflation's Impact:** Realizing that savings alone won't keep pace with rising costs, investing is crucial for maintaining and growing wealth.
- **Learning About Safe Investment Options:** Exploring diversified investments, such as index funds, bonds, and real estate, helps balance risk.
- **Starting Small:** Investing doesn't have to be overwhelming; beginning with a modest amount can build confidence.
- **Accepting Calculated Risks:** Growth necessitates stepping out of one's comfort zone while managing risk wisely.

4. The Grower Mindset: Leveraging Money for Expansion

The Grower mindset represents a transformative stage where financial security evolves into financial expansion. Unlike Savers, who focus primarily on protecting their money, Growers actively seek opportunities to make their money work for them. They recognize that wealth is not solely about how much they save but about how effectively they invest, diversify, and create additional income streams.

This stage marks a pivotal turning point, requiring a shift in thinking, the embrace of calculated risks, and a willingness to step beyond financial comfort zones.

What Makes a Grower Different?

Growers are intentional about their financial growth. They:

- **See Money as a Tool for Expansion:** They understand that money should work for them rather than merely sitting idle in a bank account.
- **Seek Multiple Income Streams:** Growers invest in stocks, real estate, businesses, or other assets that generate returns.
- **Embrace Calculated Risks:** They acknowledge that risk is necessary and mitigate it through education and strategic planning.
- **Value Mentorship and Financial Education:** They continuously seek knowledge, guidance, and refinement of their investment strategies.
- **Think Long-Term:** Their aim is not just short-term security but sustainable wealth over time.

Key Strategies of a Grower

- **Investing Wisely:** Growers explore investments such as stocks, bonds, mutual funds, real estate, and business ventures. They understand their risk tolerance and diversify their portfolios.

- **Entrepreneurship:** Many Growers initiate side businesses, freelancing, or full-scale enterprises to create additional income.
- **Reinvesting Profits:** Instead of hoarding cash, Growers reinvest their earnings into higher-yield opportunities.
- **Leveraging Networks & Mentorship:** They surround themselves with experienced mentors and financial experts to accelerate their growth.
- **Balancing Risk & Reward:** They carefully assess opportunities, ensuring that each risk taken is strategic and informed.

The Shift from Saver to Grower

I had one of my most memorable clients who was a diligent Saver, had spent years focused on financial stability, but felt frustrated. Despite having substantial savings, they felt stuck, fearing the potential losses associated with investments. Consequently, they kept their wealth in low-interest accounts, unknowingly allowing inflation to erode their savings.

After working together, they took small but significant steps toward embracing the Grower mindset:

- **Educating Themselves:** They read books, attended investment workshops, and sought mentorship to enhance their financial knowledge.
- **Starting Small:** Rather than diving into high-risk ventures, they began with low-risk index funds and dividend stocks.

- **Exploring Real Estate:** They invested in a rental property, generating passive income.
- **Launching a Side Business:** They monetized a skill, creating an additional revenue stream.

The Role of Education, Mentorship, and Calculated Risks

The Grower mindset thrives on continuous learning. Successful Growers invest in:

- **Financial Education:** Engaging in reading, taking courses, and staying updated on market trends.
- **Mentorship:** Seeking guidance from individuals who have successfully built wealth.
- **Smart Risk-Taking:** Recognizing that not every opportunity is worth pursuing, but learning to calculate risks effectively.

Transitioning to the Final Stage: The Builder Mindset

While Growers lay the foundation for long-term financial success, true financial independence comes with adopting the Builder mindset. Builders do not merely grow wealth; they create lasting financial legacies. The next step involves shifting from expanding wealth to structuring it for long-term impact.

5. The Builder Mindset: Creating Lasting Wealth and Impact

The Builder Mindset represents the pinnacle of financial evolution. Builders go beyond merely growing their wealth; they aim to create something larger than themselves. Their objective is to establish generational wealth, develop long-term businesses, and create financial systems that benefit others. This mindset transcends money; it encompasses legacy, impact, and sustainability. Builders think decades ahead, making strategic decisions that ensure their wealth endures long after they are gone.

What Defines a Builder?

Builders leverage everything they've learned as Growers to expand their influence. They:

- **Think Long-Term:** Every decision is made with the goal of sustaining wealth for future generations.
- **Focus on Legacy:** They create businesses, investment portfolios, and philanthropic ventures that leave a lasting impact.
- **Empower Others:** Builders mentor, invest in communities, and create opportunities for those around them.
- **Build Systems, Not Just Income:** They structure their wealth using trusts, foundations, and scalable businesses.
- **Develop a Financial Succession Plan:** They ensure their wealth is protected, distributed wisely, and continues to grow.

Why Builders Think Beyond Personal Wealth

At this stage, financial success is not solely about personal security; it's about making a difference. Builders ask themselves:

- How can I create wealth that lasts for generations?
- What impact can I make in my community or industry?

- How do I transition from earning to leading and mentoring?

Example of a Successful Builder

One inspiring example of a Builder is an individual who started with nothing but built a financial empire. This person:

- Began as a Saver and transitioned into a Grower by investing wisely.
- Established a scalable business that continued to thrive without their daily involvement.
- Created a trust fund to secure their children's financial future.
- Founded a charitable organization, giving back to their community.
- Developed multiple income-generating assets, ensuring financial stability for generations.

The Builder Mindset is about creating a legacy that extends beyond personal wealth, ensuring that the impact of one's financial decisions resonates for generations to come. By focusing on sustainability and empowering others, Builders lay the groundwork for a brighter financial future for themselves and their communities.

The Importance of Mentorship, Networking, and Vision

Becoming a Builder involves learning from those who have already achieved success. Key strategies for this transformation include:

- **Surrounding Yourself with High-Level Mentors and Advisors:** Builders actively seek wisdom from experienced entrepreneurs, investors, and wealth managers who can provide valuable insights and guidance.

- **Developing a Strong Financial and Legal Team:** Collaborating with estate planners, accountants, and financial advisors is essential for protecting and growing wealth effectively.

- **Networking with Like-Minded Visionaries:** Builders engage with individuals who think beyond mere financial independence and focus on creating a lasting financial legacy.

- **Creating a Vision that Extends Beyond Personal Gain:** Whether through philanthropy, leadership, or business expansion, Builders prioritize long-term impact over short-term rewards.

From Individual Wealth to a Lasting Legacy

Builders recognize that true wealth transcends money; it encompasses freedom, influence, and the ability to create opportunities for others. Their mindset undergoes a significant shift:

- **From Financial Success to Financial Significance:** They move beyond personal achievements to focus on making a meaningful difference.

- **From Personal Growth to Collective Impact:** Builders prioritize the well-being of their communities and the people around them.

- **From Making Money to Building Something That Lasts:** Their goal is to create enduring wealth, thriving businesses, and a legacy that positively impacts future generations.

The Full Financial Journey

The five money mindsets—Survivor, Spender, Saver, Grower, and Builder—illustrate an evolving financial path. Recognizing your current mindset is the essential first step toward progressing to the next level.

- Survivors work tirelessly to escape financial instability.
- Spenders focus on controlling their impulses and developing financial discipline.
- Savers prioritize protecting their money but must learn to embrace growth opportunities.
- Growers actively expand their wealth by taking calculated risks.
- Builders strive to create long-term wealth, making a significant impact and leaving a lasting legacy.

Each stage demands shifts in mindset, continuous learning, and decisive action. The ultimate aim is not merely financial success but achieving financial mastery and building a legacy that endures.

6. The Transformation Process: Moving from One Mindset to the Next

Transitioning through the five money mindsets—Survivor, Spender, Saver, Grower, and Builder—is not an overnight process. It demands self-awareness, discipline, and a willingness to change. Each stage presents unique challenges, but with the right mindset shifts and strategies, financial growth becomes possible for anyone.

Recognizing Your Current Mindset and Embracing Change

The first step in this transformative journey is honest self-reflection. Ask yourself:

- Do I struggle to cover my basic needs? → You may be in the Survivor stage.
- Do I frequently spend on wants rather than needs? → You might be a Spender.
- Am I focused on saving but hesitant to take risks? → You likely have a Saver mindset.
- Am I actively looking for ways to grow my wealth? → You're in the Grower stage.
- Am I building lasting wealth and opportunities for others? → You've reached the Builder mindset.

The Challenges of Moving from One Phase to Another

Each transition comes with specific hurdles that must be overcome:

- **Survivor → Spender:** The biggest challenge is breaking the scarcity mindset. Survivors often fear spending any money, even on essentials. The key is gaining financial stability first—building an emergency fund, eliminating high-interest debt, and creating a basic budget.
- **Spender → Saver:** Spenders struggle with instant gratification and emotional spending. The shift requires

mindful budgeting, distinguishing wants from needs, and understanding the long-term impact of financial choices.

- **Saver → Grower:** Savers typically have a fear of risk and prefer security over opportunity. To transition, they must embrace financial education, start small with investing, and understand that wealth growth requires calculated risks.
- **Grower → Builder:** Growers must learn that wealth isn't just about personal gain—it's about creating systems that generate financial security for the future. The challenge is thinking beyond short-term profits and focusing on sustainability, leadership, and impact.

The Personal Fulfillment of Helping Others on This Journey

Guiding people through these financial transformations has been one of the most rewarding experiences. Witnessing someone go from barely surviving to building lasting wealth is proof that financial success is possible for anyone willing to learn and take action.

I've seen clients:

- Escape the paycheck-to-paycheck cycle and regain financial control.
- Break free from impulsive spending and achieve true financial discipline.
- Overcome fear and hesitation to invest in their future.
- Grow businesses and create financial opportunities for others.
- Build generational wealth and leave a meaningful legacy.

Financial Growth Is About Willingness to Evolve

Your financial journey is not defined by where you start—it's shaped by your willingness to learn, adapt, and grow.

- Success isn't about how much money you have now—it's about the habits and mindset you develop.
- Each stage of financial growth requires new skills, new perspectives, and new strategies.
- The path to wealth isn't just about making more money—it's about using it wisely, multiplying it, and making an impact.

Chapter Three: Survival Mode: The Fight For Stability

Understanding Survival Mode

Survival mode is a state where every decision is driven by immediate needs rather than long-term aspirations. It involves the constant strain of living paycheck to paycheck, making choices based on short-term relief instead of future stability. When someone is caught in survival mode, they aren't thinking about investments, personal growth, or long-term success; their focus is solely on making it through the day, week, or month. This reactive approach can trap individuals in a cycle of financial and emotional struggle, obscuring opportunities for genuine progress.

One of the most significant challenges posed by survival mode is its detrimental effect on mindset. When your attention is solely on short-term survival, envisioning a different reality becomes incredibly difficult. Dreams of financial independence, career growth, or personal fulfillment may seem distant—if not entirely unattainable. However, the key to breaking free from survival mode begins in the mind. The way you perceive your circumstances and possibilities can either keep you stuck or propel you toward a breakthrough.

This concept is often highlighted in success and personal development literature. For instance, The Secret popularized the idea that "what the mind can imagine, you can achieve." This philosophy posits that by focusing on positive outcomes and genuinely believing in them, individuals can attract success into their lives. While there is merit to the power of belief, it is only part of the equation. Positive thinking alone is insufficient; action is essential. You can't simply wish your way out of survival mode; you must take intentional steps to change your situation.

In this chapter, I will share my journey of breaking free from survival mode, the mindset shifts that enabled me to move forward, and the practical steps anyone can take to achieve the same. It all starts with belief, but it requires strategy, discipline, and persistence to create lasting change.

The Reality of Survival Mode: My Personal Journey

Starting a business while trapped in survival mode was one of the toughest decisions I ever faced. When you're struggling to pay bills, the thought of investing time and energy into something that won't bring immediate financial relief feels incredibly risky—almost irresponsible. Every instinct urges you to play it safe, accept the guaranteed paycheck, and put your dreams on hold. However, I realized that without taking a chance, I would remain stuck in that same cycle forever.

I vividly recall a conversation with my mom during that challenging period. She noticed my struggles and suggested I get a fast-food job for a steady income. She wasn't wrong—taking that job would have provided instant relief. A paycheck every two weeks could have covered rent, groceries, and some debt. Yet, I also understood that accepting that job would mean indefinitely postponing my business aspirations. I faced a pivotal choice: pursue the short-term fix or endure temporary hardship for the sake of long-term success.

Making that choice wasn't easy. There were days when I doubted myself, especially when money was tight and the stress felt overwhelming. However, I held onto my vision, reminding myself that sacrifice was essential for growth. I cut expenses, worked long hours, and remained dedicated to building something greater than just another paycheck-to-paycheck existence.

The outcome? Within a year, I had saved enough for a down payment on a house. The very thing that once seemed impossible—owning property and achieving financial stability—became a reality because I refused to let survival mode dictate my future. That experience taught me that escaping survival mode requires taking calculated risks, believing in your long-term vision, and staying committed, even when short-term struggles feel unbearable.

The Trap of Surrounding Yourself with the Wrong People

One of the most significant obstacles to breaking free from survival mode is the company you keep. It's no coincidence that people who are struggling to get ahead often surround themselves with others who are also stuck. Misery loves company, and when everyone around you is merely trying to get by, it's easy to believe that this is all life has to offer.

I've witnessed this firsthand—friends and acquaintances who would spend every conversation complaining about their circumstances without ever taking action to change them. They reinforced the belief that struggle was inevitable, that opportunities were scarce, and that anyone who attempted to do better was either lucky or bound to fail. When I began shifting my mindset and focusing on building a business, I noticed resistance from some of the people around me. They questioned my decisions, doubted my success, and sometimes even laughed at my ambitions.

That's when I realized something crucial: not everyone wants to see you succeed. Some people cling to their survival mindset because it's familiar, and when they observe someone breaking free, it forces them to confront their own limitations. Instead of feeling inspired, they often become resentful.

To genuinely escape survival mode, you must be intentional about the people you allow into your life. Surround yourself with those who believe in growth, challenge you to think bigger, and support your journey. If you consistently engage with individuals who only see obstacles, you'll start to believe that success is out of reach. Conversely, spending time with those who see possibilities can help you cultivate that same belief.

Breaking free isn't just about changing your actions—it's about transforming your environment. If the people around you drain your energy, reinforce a scarcity mindset, or discourage your dreams, it may be time to distance yourself. Growth requires sacrifice, and sometimes that means letting go of relationships that no longer serve your future.

Education as a Path to Escape

Breaking free from survival mode requires more than just hard work—it demands knowledge. Unfortunately, traditional education systems often operate on outdated models that teach skills that may not be relevant in today's fast-paced world. Schools tend to emphasize rote memorization and standardized testing, failing to equip students with essential practical skills such as financial literacy, critical thinking, and entrepreneurship.

Consider artificial intelligence (AI) as an example. AI now possesses an estimated IQ ranging from 500 to 1000, significantly surpassing human intelligence in data processing and analysis. While many fear that AI will eliminate jobs, those who learn to leverage it can gain a tremendous advantage. Tools like ChatGPT, automation software, and machine learning can level the playing field, enabling individuals to compete with major corporations, scale businesses, and make informed decisions based on data-driven insights. Yet, most schools do not teach students how to effectively utilize AI.

This underscores the importance of self-education. To escape survival mode, you must take responsibility for your own learning. Traditional schooling serves as a foundation, but the real education begins when you actively seek knowledge that aligns with your goals. Books, online courses, mentorship, and hands-on experience are invaluable resources.

For me, books played a pivotal role in shifting my mindset. Reading Think and Grow Rich by Napoleon Hill opened my eyes to the power of thought and persistence. Similarly, Rich Dad Poor Dad and Cashflow Quadrant by Robert Kiyosaki reshaped my perception of money, demonstrating that financial freedom is more about working smarter than working harder. These books provided practical insights that I applied to both my life and my business.

The key is to find resources that resonate with you. Not every book or course will be a perfect fit, but continuous learning will always propel you forward. In the digital age, there's no excuse for ignorance—valuable knowledge is readily available at little to no cost. By investing in your education, you'll equip yourself with the tools necessary to break free from survival mode and build a brighter future.

The Importance of Skill Development and Opportunity Seeking

One of the most significant misconceptions holding people back is the belief that a degree is essential for success. While formal education can certainly open doors, it is not the only path to financial stability or career advancement. In today's world, skills often outweigh credentials. Many successful entrepreneurs, freelancers, and industry leaders never completed college; they thrived by developing valuable skills and proactively seeking opportunities.

Employers are increasingly prioritizing attitude, adaptability, and problem-solving abilities over formal degrees. A prime example is the story of a coffee shop worker who was hired as an intern at a tech company. Despite lacking formal education in the field, she demonstrated a strong work ethic and a genuine eagerness to learn. Within months, she received on-the-job training, developed industry-relevant skills, and eventually secured a full-time position. This illustrates that the right mindset and willingness to learn can create opportunities, even in competitive industries.

However, skill development alone isn't sufficient—you also need to actively seek out opportunities. This is where networking becomes a game-changer. Too often, people assume opportunities will come to them, but the reality is that you must put yourself out there. Communicate your goals and aspirations to others. Attend industry events, join online communities, connect with mentors, and cultivate relationships.

Many opportunities are not advertised—they often emerge from conversations, recommendations, and being in the right place at the right time. Someone in your network might know about an opening, a freelance gig, or a business opportunity that aligns with your skills. But if no one is aware of what you're seeking, those opportunities may slip away.

Breaking free from survival mode involves shifting from a passive mindset to a proactive one. Rather than waiting for circumstances to improve, focus on building your skills, creating opportunities, and leveraging your network. The more you develop your abilities and immerse yourself in the right circles, the faster you'll progress toward financial freedom and long-term success.

The Role of Discipline and Personal Habits

Discipline is the cornerstone of long-term success. Whether in business, finances, or personal growth, success is not the product of sporadic actions; it results from consistent, disciplined habits. The principle that how you do one thing is how you do everything signifies that discipline in one area of life often translates to success in others.

A compelling example of this is maintaining discipline in personal health. Imagine committing to running every day, regardless of the weather or how you feel. Over time, this habit cultivates mental toughness, demonstrating that you can push through discomfort and remain committed to your goals. That same discipline extends into financial and career success—showing up consistently, doing the hard work even when you lack motivation, and staying focused on the bigger picture.

Building discipline begins with small, intentional habits. Here are a few that reinforce a growth mindset:

- **Morning routines:** Starting the day with intention—whether through reading, exercise, or meditation—sets a productive tone for the rest of the day.
- **Financial discipline:** Saving consistently, investing wisely, and avoiding unnecessary expenses are habits that lead to financial independence.
- **Continuous learning:** Engaging with books, listening to podcasts, and staying informed about new opportunities fosters a mindset of constant improvement.
- **Time management:** Prioritizing tasks and eliminating distractions helps maximize efficiency and progress toward long-term goals.

It's important to note that discipline isn't about perfection—it's about showing up daily, even when motivation wanes. Motivation may get you started, but discipline keeps you going. The ability to build and maintain positive habits is what distinguishes those who break free from survival mode from those who remain trapped in it.

Conclusion: A Mindset Shift Leads to Action

Breaking free from survival mode isn't merely about desiring a better life—it demands both a shift in mindset and consistent action. Many people find themselves stuck because they believe they have no other choice, but the truth is that change is always possible. The key is to take control of what you can, no matter how small the first step may seem.

Practical Steps to Breaking Free

1. Stay Away from Negative Influences

The people around you can either inspire growth or keep you trapped in a cycle of scarcity.

- Be intentional about your circle—surround yourself with individuals who uplift, challenge, and encourage your progress.
- Distance yourself from those who drain your energy, discourage your ambitions, or reinforce limiting beliefs.

2. Commit to Self-Education

Traditional education doesn't always prepare people for real-world success.

- Invest in learning—read books, take online courses, and study skills that open doors to new opportunities.
- Remember that knowledge is power, and in today's world, access to information is virtually limitless.

3. Seek Opportunities and Network

Many doors open simply by letting others know you're looking for opportunities.

- Don't hesitate to reach out, ask for advice, or immerse yourself in environments where opportunities abound.
- Build relationships with individuals who are already where you aspire to be.

4. Develop Self-Discipline in All Areas of Life

Discipline is the bridge between goals and achievements.

- Small, daily habits—such as maintaining financial discipline, prioritizing your health, and committing to personal growth—lead to long-term success.
- The more consistent you are, the more momentum you build.

Take the First Step Today

The biggest mistake people make is waiting for the "perfect time" to start. There is no perfect time; the perfect time is now. Even the smallest actions—reading a book, reaching out to a mentor, or setting a financial goal—can initiate the momentum that leads to transformation.

The journey out of survival mode may not be easy, but it is undoubtedly worth it. The moment you decide to think bigger, take action, and commit to growth, you begin to create a better future for yourself. Your success starts today.

Chapter Four: The Spender's World: Chasing Instant Gratification

"The greatest investment you can make is in yourself."

-Philip Fisher.

The Spender's Dilemma: Breaking the Cycle for Financial Security

Recently, I had an interesting conversation with a friend whose husband is eager to start a business. He often mentions needing a specific amount of money to kick things off—money that could be saved if he simply cut down on his spending. My friend made a poignant observation: they always seem to have funds for outings, yet saving for the business appears out of reach. This highlights a widespread issue: spending becomes an excuse that prevents people from pursuing new ventures.

For many, the true fear lies not in a lack of funds but in the accountability that comes with having resources. When they possess the money, they must take action and make it work. Without it, they have a convenient excuse for not chasing their dreams. This mindset is understandable; starting something new often brings a wave of fear—fear of failure, fear of the unknown, and fear of the effort required. However, as discussed earlier, a steadfast belief in oneself and optimism are crucial for success. The same principle applies to financial habits: if you identify as a spender, only you can alter your habits, but it starts with believing that change is possible.

Understanding the Spender Mindset

Breaking away from the spender mentality can occur in two primary ways: either by curbing unnecessary expenses or by increasing income to outpace spending. The latter option is often more challenging, as many who boost their income simply escalate their spending—purchasing bigger, better, and more luxurious items. This cycle continues unless conscious efforts are made to disrupt it.

Spending habits are frequently rooted in past experiences. Individuals raised in financially constrained environments may have been repeatedly told, “We can’t afford that.” As adults, they might resist saying, “I can’t afford it,” leading them to spend as a means of avoiding discomfort. Social media further complicates this issue, as people are constantly bombarded with images of others enjoying extravagant lifestyles, often overlooking whether those individuals are genuinely financially secure or grappling with debt.

Many people transition from survival mode—struggling to make ends meet—to a spender mentality upon receiving extra income. They justify their expenses by believing they deserve rewards for their hard work, neglecting the importance of establishing financial security for the future.

The Consequences of the Spender Mindset

A notable example of the spender mentality is observed in individuals who contribute to pensions and 401(k) plans but frequently borrow against them. While they may save, they simultaneously drain those savings, jeopardizing long-term financial security. This lack of discipline traps them in a cycle of consuming every dollar they earn.

To escape this mindset, self-awareness and discipline are essential. Many possess a financial "vice"—a daily expense that offers short-term satisfaction yet undermines long-term goals. This could manifest as spending on coffee, dining out, shopping, or entertainment. These small, frequent indulgences accumulate, making it challenging to build savings. Often, this spending serves as a form of self-medication for the stress associated with financial struggles.

Another critical element is social influence. Being surrounded by individuals who also spend recklessly makes it significantly harder to adopt a saver mindset. Conversely, associating with financially disciplined people can motivate and hold one accountable for making wiser financial choices.

Financial Security and Relationships

Spending habits significantly impact relationships, especially in marriages. Women, in particular, often seek financial stability along with emotional and physical security. This desire for financial security does not imply that they only care about money; rather, it provides a sense of safety and predictability. Historically, women relied on men for financial support during pregnancy or child-rearing, making financial security a deeply ingrained need.

While some women may choose to be financially independent, it remains vital for both partners to adopt a responsible approach to money. A man who spends recklessly may struggle to attract a serious partner, while a woman who is perpetually broke may be unfairly viewed as financially dependent. Ultimately, financial stability benefits both partners and fosters a healthier relationship dynamic.

Breaking Free from the Spender Cycle

To transition from a spender mindset to a saver mindset, consider these steps:

- **Identify Your Spending Triggers** – Understand what prompts you to spend unnecessarily and discover healthier alternatives to address those emotions.
- **Track Your Expenses** – Awareness is the first step towards control. Keep a detailed record of all your spending for at least one month.
- **Set Financial Goals** – Whether it's launching a business, purchasing a home, or retiring early, having clear goals helps maintain discipline.
- **Surround Yourself with Savers** – Engage with individuals who have sound financial habits and learn from their experiences.
- **Automate Savings** – Establish automatic transfers to savings accounts, making saving effortless.

- **Shift Your Mindset** – Replace "I can't afford it" with "How can I afford it?" This small change fosters creativity and problem-solving rather than resignation.

Financial issues are one of the leading causes of divorce. The stress associated with money can create emotional distance between partners, leading to dissatisfaction and, in some instances, infidelity. A partner in this situation may feel both financially and emotionally insecure but struggle to express these concerns.

Living paycheck to paycheck, even with a higher income, often equates to financial survival. Although one might afford better food and clothing, the underlying reality remains unchanged—there is little to no financial security. Many families grapple with this challenge, as inflation erodes their income, leaving minimal room for discretionary spending. This strain is particularly challenging for families with children, as childcare expenses further complicate their financial situation.

So, how can families facing these difficulties change their circumstances?

One of the most effective tools available is education. Even amid financial hardship, most individuals have access to the internet, whether through a smartphone or computer. This access allows them to seek out resources, learn new skills, and make informed financial decisions.

For instance, small changes in spending habits can lead to significant savings. Take the cost of home Wi-Fi as an example. If eliminating this expense saves $120 a month, that money can be redirected toward essential needs. Many mobile phone plans include data that can serve as an alternative to internet access. While Wi-Fi is commonly viewed as a necessity, it can often be considered a luxury compared to using mobile data.

The key to financial improvement lies in self-determination. Even minor adjustments can help break the cycle of financial strain. However, for those who have been in this situation for an extended period, believing that change is possible may be challenging. Some might argue that cutting expenses is easier said than done, and while this viewpoint is understandable, achieving financial security often requires making difficult decisions.

For example, cable television can be seen as an unnecessary expense when more affordable entertainment options are available through streaming services. Yet, many people who cancel cable end up subscribing to multiple streaming services, ultimately spending just as much as before. Being mindful of these spending habits and eliminating unnecessary expenses is crucial for achieving financial stability.

Breaking the Cycle of Spending and Achieving Financial Freedom

Many individuals find themselves caught in a cycle of spending, often confusing "spender mode" for financial freedom, when in reality, they are merely surviving. This distinction is crucial, as those who believe they are simply enjoying their earnings may be just one unexpected expense away from financial distress.

When receiving a raise or unexpected financial windfall, a common question arises: is it better to upgrade one's lifestyle, invest in financial markets, or focus on personal growth? The answer is not universal, but investing in oneself frequently yields the highest returns. Education—whether through formal degrees, online courses, or self-directed study—can provide long-term financial benefits. For instance, someone considering stock market investments would benefit from first understanding fundamental financial principles before committing their money.

Another significant form of investment is personal presentation, which can greatly influence professional advancement. A compelling example is of an individual who lost a substantial amount of weight but neglected to update his wardrobe. Despite his intelligence and capability, his ill-fitting clothes conveyed an impression of disregard, ultimately hindering his chances for promotion. Simple changes, such as dressing appropriately and maintaining a professional appearance, can significantly affect how one is perceived and open new opportunities.

Financial discipline is essential for escaping the paycheck-to-paycheck cycle. While rewarding oneself for hard work is important, a balanced approach is necessary. Instead of making drastic lifestyle changes—like purchasing an expensive car with overwhelming payments—it is wiser to save strategically and indulge in well-deserved rewards, such as travel or updating one's wardrobe.

Unfortunately, many people reach their 40s or 50s without breaking free from financial instability. While change is possible at any stage, the longer one remains in spender mode, the more challenging it becomes to escape. Those burdened with excessive debt may even face the daunting prospect of bankruptcy. While bankruptcy can offer a fresh start for some, repeatedly relying on it indicates a failure to learn from past mistakes. For those determined to avoid such outcomes, strict budgeting and disciplined spending adjustments—like canceling unnecessary subscriptions—can pave the way to financial stability.

Adjusting Financial Approaches for Adoption

For my wife and me, adopting our children later in life required a shift in our financial mindset. I became a father in my early 40s, and my children have never heard the phrase, "We can't afford that." Instead, we use the expression, "It's not in the budget." This change in language is powerful; it moves away from a mindset of limitation and perceived failure, promoting financial maturity and responsibility.

When you say, "I can't afford it," it suggests a lack of financial means. In contrast, saying, "It's not in the budget," implies that you have a plan and are making intentional financial decisions. This approach not only fosters respect from those around you but may also inspire discussions about financial discipline and budgeting strategies.

The Importance of Budgeting

To create a solid financial plan, start by assessing where every dollar goes. List all your monthly expenses and categorize them into three distinct groups:

- **A - Absolute Necessities:** These are essential expenses such as rent or mortgage, groceries, utilities, car payments, and insurance. These items are non-negotiable.
- **B - Important but Optional:** These include expenses like internet service, premium phone plans, or gym memberships. While not essential, they add value to your life and well-being.
- **C - Luxuries and Non-Essentials:** These are discretionary expenses, such as dining out, entertainment, high-end beauty treatments, or frequent shopping sprees. While enjoyable, they are not necessary for basic survival or well-being.

By carefully categorizing your spending, you gain clarity on where your money goes. Many people unknowingly allocate too much to category C and misclassify category B items as necessities when, in reality, they belong in category C.

Reallocating Funds for Financial Stability

For example, if your monthly income is $6,000 and you find that you're spending $2,000 on non-essential luxuries, consider reallocating those funds. Instead of allowing category C to consume such a large portion of your budget, redirect that money toward necessities like paying off debt or increasing savings. Here's how:

If you shift part of your luxury spending to an accelerated car payment plan, you can pay off your vehicle sooner, eliminating a fixed expense.

Once you eliminate a significant necessity like a car payment, you can redirect those funds toward investments, emergency savings, or future large purchases, such as a home.

Practical Budgeting Strategies

One effective way to ensure financial discipline is to involve a trusted friend in your budgeting process. Share your budgets with each other and critique where cuts could be made. This exercise provides an outside perspective and introduces accountability. When you need to justify spending $200 a month on a high-end gym instead of a $60 alternative or why you choose professional hair coloring over embracing your natural shade, it forces you to reflect on your financial priorities.

Maximizing Everyday Expenses

If you must spend money, find ways to make it work for you. Many credit cards, like the BILT card, allow for rent payments without additional fees while earning rewards. Similarly, using reward programs on necessary purchases, such as gas or groceries, can lead to long-term savings. For instance, some fuel stations offer double points on specific days, which can translate into significant discounts over time. Using these points wisely, particularly during costly road trips, can have a substantial financial impact.

The Power of Mindset in Achieving Financial Success

Mindset is arguably the most crucial factor in attaining financial success. When I launched my business, I started with nothing more than a computer and a borrowed desk in the front room of a rented house. Nevertheless, I held a firm belief that one day, I would earn a million dollars in a single year. I committed to that goal for 20 years, unwavering in my determination. The journey was not linear—there were years filled with setbacks, and times when my earnings dipped. Yet, I remained resolute. Ultimately, I not only reached that milestone but exceeded it, accumulating millions along the way.

Success is not a product of wishful thinking; it requires action. The key difference between those who hope to become wealthy and those who actually achieve it lies in their level of commitment and the proactive steps they take. It's insufficient to merely desire financial success; one must actively pursue it with a structured plan.

Breaking Down the Timeline for Success

One of the most significant challenges people face is their perception of time. If someone is currently earning a modest income and is challenged to make a million dollars in a year, they might find that goal laughable. However, by breaking it down into achievable milestones, it becomes a more realistic target.

For instance, rather than focusing on making a million dollars immediately, one might aim to double their income over the next three years. This involves identifying actionable steps—whether that means working additional hours, securing a better job, switching careers, or starting a business. A more manageable target could be increasing income by 20% each year. Over three years, this results in a 60% increase. Maintaining this momentum over time can lead to significant financial growth, ultimately leading to that million-dollar goal.

Smart Financial Management and Diversification

Financial success involves more than just earning money; it requires wise management. Many individuals work hard to accumulate wealth, only to watch it disappear when they stop investing effort. To prevent this, it's essential to take profits and invest them in long-term, stable assets that generate ongoing income.

Consider the fluctuations in markets—Bitcoin, for instance, dropped over 20% in the last month, while the stock market experienced volatility but remained relatively stable. A wise investor would consider diversifying their portfolio. If Bitcoin reaches a high point, it may be prudent to sell a portion of those holdings and reinvest in other assets, such as stocks, real estate, or even a savings account that offers steady returns. The goal is to create multiple streams of income rather than relying solely on one volatile source.

Expanding Income Streams

Diversification should extend beyond investments; it should also encompass income streams. Depending on a single source of income—whether it's a job, trading, or a single business—can be risky. Instead, individuals should seek additional opportunities, such as starting a side business, freelancing, or investing in passive income sources like rental properties. A robust financial foundation is built on multiple income streams that provide both stability and growth over time.

By adopting the right mindset, setting realistic milestones, managing finances wisely, and diversifying income sources, anyone can create sustainable wealth. It's not about making quick money; it's about crafting a long-term financial strategy that ensures lasting success.

Easy Come, Easy Go: The Truth About Wealth Building

It's all too easy to become ensnared by the illusion of effortless success, particularly when scrolling through social media. While some individuals portray their journeys as simple, the reality is often much different. Years ago, I was advised to establish a presence on LinkedIn as a financial advisor. A popular narrative mentioned an advisor who made a single connection that transformed his career. However, in all my years, I've only encountered that one success story.

I know hundreds of financial advisors, and very few have built a lucrative business solely through LinkedIn. This isn't to discredit the platform; it's a valuable tool. However, if your entire strategy hinges on it, you must be fully committed. Too many people pursue quick and easy wealth, but such options are largely illusory. The harder something is to achieve, the more likely it is to be sustainable.

The Investment of Time and Effort

Consider the time and energy many individuals invest in Bitcoin or other speculative ventures. What if that same effort were applied to building a business? Imagine dedicating yourself to launching and growing a company, with the potential to sell it down the line. Not only would you earn a living along the way, but you would also create jobs and contribute something valuable to the world. The long-term rewards could be far greater, and you would have built something meaningful.

This isn't to suggest avoiding Bitcoin or other online opportunities entirely, but they shouldn't comprise your entire strategy. Many so-called "gurus" on platforms like YouTube and social media generate income not from the businesses they promote, but from selling courses about those businesses. Before investing in their promises, ask yourself: Are they truly making a living from the thing they teach, or are they profiting from selling you a dream?

The Hidden Costs of Get-Rich-Quick Schemes

People often spend $10,000 to $15,000 on courses that promise financial success, yet the actual success rate is frequently less than 1%. When those investments don't yield results, blame often shifts to the student—"You chose the wrong product." But with those odds, the issue lies with the system itself.

Now, imagine taking that same $10,000 to $15,000 and using it to start a hands-on business. You could lease a vehicle and start a mobile car wash, charging $40 per car, with just 100 clients, that could generate $4,000 in revenue. Over time, you could hire employees, scale the business, and eventually sell it. That's real wealth—building something sustainable instead of chasing quick fixes.

The Value of Persistence and Hard Work

Making money isn't easy; it requires hard work. While some individuals earn millions on platforms like YouTube or OnlyFans, those are exceptions, not the norm. Even in those industries, long-term success demands financial wisdom and reinvestment.

Consider YouTube influencers: none of them started with millions of followers. Their success is a product of years of consistency and persistence. I remember my kids watching EvanTube when they were younger. His initial videos were simple, likely filmed by his father on a phone. Over time, that modest channel evolved into a multimillion-dollar operation, complete with production staff and brand partnerships. But it didn't happen overnight; it took years of dedicated effort.

A Different Way of Thinking

Optimism, commitment, and persistence are essential. Instead of pursuing easy money, navigate life with your eyes open and seek real opportunities. These opportunities don't have to be on YouTube, Amazon, or social media. While those paths may work for some, countless opportunities exist right in front of us.

Sometimes, you may need to work for free before seeing returns. I've found myself in situations where I managed payroll and was the only one left unpaid. But that's part of building something authentic. The real question isn't just how to make money, but how to create something that lasts.

Chapter Five: The Saver's Discipline

From Budgeting to Saving: The Next Essential Step

Once you've established a solid budget and gained control over your expenses, the next crucial step is learning to save. While budgeting helps you track where your money goes, saving gives that money a purpose—one that benefits your future. This progression in your financial journey marks a shift from merely surviving paycheck to paycheck to actively creating a safety net for yourself.

Many people make the mistake of waiting until they are completely debt-free before considering saving. While this approach may seem rational, it often traps you in a precarious cycle. Without savings, any unexpected expense—be it a car repair, a medical bill, or even a job loss—can quickly plunge you back into debt. It's akin to trying to climb out of a hole while someone continuously dumps dirt back in.

This is why saving while also paying off debt is not just wise—it's essential. Even small contributions to your savings can significantly alter your relationship with money. It creates a buffer between you and potential crises, allowing you to rest easier at night knowing you have options. This isn't merely about financial security; it also brings a sense of psychological peace.

The reality is that emergencies are inevitable. Life is unpredictable. The important question isn't whether something will go wrong, but rather when it will happen. By saving while you pay down debt, you ensure that the next disruption doesn't devastate your finances. It's about achieving stability, building confidence, and refusing to let a temporary setback become a long-term struggle.

You don't have to wait until you're completely debt-free to start saving—in fact, you shouldn't. The two efforts should go hand in hand. Approach your debt repayment with discipline, but also honor your future self by setting aside a little money every month. This practice embodies the saver's discipline, and it's the key to getting ahead.

Understanding the Saver Mindset

The saver mindset is fundamentally anchored in the pursuit of financial security and stability. It emphasizes the importance of setting aside resources for future needs, focusing on long-term goals rather than immediate pleasures. This mindset is not about being overly frugal or constantly fretting over every expenditure; it's about being proactive and prioritizing delayed gratification. Savers recognize that the sacrifices they make today in saving and budgeting will ultimately lead to a more secure future.

At its essence, the saver mindset is about creating a safety net that provides comfort amid uncertainty. For savers, having a robust emergency fund brings a profound sense of psychological relief. It's not just the tangible security of having money in the bank; it's the emotional freedom that comes from knowing you won't be thrown off course by unexpected events. It's the peace of mind that allows you to choose your next steps rather than react out of panic or necessity.

This mindset not only offers peace of mind but also nurtures confidence. When you know your savings are available to support you, you're less likely to feel paralyzed by life's challenges. Whether it's an urgent home repair, a medical bill, or even a temporary job loss, savers feel empowered because they have anticipated these hurdles and prepared for them.

However, the saver mindset does come with its contradictions, particularly regarding risk. While the safety net of savings provides a comforting sense of security, it can also create hesitation around taking financial risks. For many savers, the thought of investing or starting a business can be intimidating. There's often a fear of losing what they have carefully accumulated—a concern that those hard-earned dollars could diminish in a risky endeavor.

This aversion to risk can lead to tension between financial growth and financial preservation. Opportunities for greater financial success often require stepping outside one's comfort zone—whether through investing in the stock market, real estate, or entrepreneurship. Yet, these opportunities come with the potential for loss, making the trade-off feel daunting for someone with a saver mindset.

The challenge, then, lies in finding a balance between safeguarding savings for security and remaining open to opportunities that encourage growth. The key is to understand that pursuing financial growth doesn't have to equate to reckless risk-taking. There are strategic ways to build wealth—such as investing in diversified portfolios, educating oneself about business ventures, or gradually exploring calculated risks—that still allow for a solid safety net.

The Three-Pronged Approach to Financial Security

Achieving a comprehensive financial strategy requires more than just one element; it involves crafting a balanced approach that addresses both immediate needs and long-term aspirations. A three-pronged approach to financial security provides a structured framework for managing your finances across various time frames, ensuring both stability and growth. This strategy encompasses short-term liquidity, medium-term growth, and long-term planning, with each component serving a distinct purpose in your overall financial landscape.

Short-Term Liquidity: Emergency Savings

The cornerstone of financial security is short-term liquidity—having ready access to cash for unexpected expenses. Life is unpredictable, and a well-funded emergency savings account is crucial for maintaining your financial peace of mind. Ideally, this account should be easily accessible, allowing for quick withdrawals when you need them most.

It's generally recommended to have at least one month's worth of living expenses set aside in a liquid savings account. This cushion acts as your first line of defense against emergencies, whether it's an urgent medical bill, a car repair, or an unexpected job loss. By establishing this safety net, you can avoid relying on credit cards or loans during a crisis, which can quickly lead to debt.

When deciding how much to save, consider your individual circumstances. Families or those with higher living costs may need a larger buffer, while individuals with fewer responsibilities might start with a smaller amount. The key is consistency—prioritize funding this account before allocating money to other investments. Only after securing this immediate financial cushion should you explore additional saving strategies.

Medium-Term Growth: Accessible Investments

Once your emergency savings are in place, the next step is to focus on medium-term growth. This category includes goals that are neither urgent nor distant, such as saving for a home down payment, funding a child's education, or building a travel fund. The objective here is to invest money in a way that provides moderate growth while keeping the funds accessible.

One effective method for achieving medium-term growth is through taxable investment accounts, particularly mutual funds. Unlike retirement accounts (like IRAs or 401(k)s), these accounts are not subject to withdrawal restrictions or penalties, offering flexibility to access your funds when necessary while still benefiting from growth over time.

Regular contributions to these accounts, even in small amounts, can significantly impact your financial future. By selecting a diversified mix of mutual funds, you can balance risk while pursuing reasonable growth. For those with a longer time horizon—say 5 to 10 years—medium-term investments are ideal for building wealth without the urgency of short-term savings accounts.

As a guideline, aim to consistently contribute a percentage of your monthly income into these accounts. Like any investment, it's essential to periodically reassess your goals and adjust your strategy as needed.

Long-Term Planning: Retirement Contributions

The final prong of financial security focuses on the long term—retirement planning. Employer-sponsored retirement accounts, such as a 401(k), are among the most effective tools for ensuring long-term financial stability. These accounts offer tax advantages, and many employers match a portion of your contributions, making them vital for wealth accumulation over time.

While contributing to retirement accounts is crucial, it's important to avoid becoming "retirement rich, cash poor." This situation occurs when a significant portion of your wealth is tied up in retirement accounts, leaving you with little to no accessible savings for emergencies or unexpected events. The challenge is that retirement savings cannot be accessed without penalties before a certain age (typically 59½), which can create difficulties if you face a financial emergency beforehand.

To maintain balance, ensure that while you contribute to retirement accounts, you also prioritize short-term and medium-term savings. You don't want to find yourself in a position where your wealth is locked away in retirement accounts, leaving you without the liquidity needed for immediate needs. The key is to actively contribute to retirement while ensuring you have accessible funds for pressing financial situations.

A Holistic Strategy for Stability

This three-pronged approach offers a well-rounded strategy for managing personal finances. By addressing short-term liquidity, medium-term growth, and long-term planning, you set yourself up for a life of financial stability, growth, and confidence. While it may seem like a lot of work upfront, this holistic approach provides the flexibility needed to adapt to life's changes while safeguarding against the unexpected.

The Importance of Emergency Funds and Strategic Financial Planning

Life can be unpredictable—whether it's an unexpected job loss, a medical emergency, or a car breakdown, having cash on hand can make a world of difference. While the term "emergency" often brings to mind catastrophic events, it's crucial to recognize that many such situations can be anticipated and managed with proper planning. By shifting our mindset, we can treat potential disruptions as manageable aspects of life rather than overwhelming crises.

Why Emergency Funds Are Vital

An emergency fund acts as a financial safety net, specifically set aside for life's inevitable disruptions. This fund ensures that you won't have to rely on credit cards, loans, or borrowing from friends and family when unexpected expenses arise. Instead, you can address these issues without jeopardizing your financial stability or compromising your long-term goals.

The primary aim of an emergency fund is to cover unexpected events that disrupt your income flow, allowing you to handle them without derailing your finances. Ideally, this fund should be kept separate from regular savings or investment accounts, preferably in a high-yield savings account for easy access without temptation.

Most financial advisors recommend saving at least 3 to 6 months' worth of living expenses. This amount can vary based on your personal situation, but the goal is to have enough to cover essentials like rent, utilities, and food in case your income is interrupted. This fund provides peace of mind, knowing you're protected against job loss, illness, or other significant setbacks.

Rethinking Emergencies

Instead of viewing emergencies as rare and catastrophic events, consider them as predictable occurrences in life. Expenses like car repairs, medical bills, home maintenance, and rent increases can often be anticipated with proper planning.

For example, everyone knows that a car will need maintenance eventually. Rather than waiting for a breakdown, setting aside a small amount each month for vehicle expenses can make these costs manageable. Similarly, rent increases are common, especially in urban areas. By forecasting potential changes, you can plan ahead and avoid surprises.

With an emergency fund established, these disruptions become manageable rather than overwhelming. You can confidently handle unexpected expenses without sacrificing your financial health.

Real-Life Examples of Predictable "Emergencies"

- **Car Maintenance:** Owning a car means it will require repairs. Regularly setting aside a small amount for maintenance can help you avoid panic when it's time for repairs, ensuring you're not forced to rely on credit cards.
- **Medical Expenses:** Health-related emergencies can be financially stressful. By saving for medical costs in advance—whether through a Health Savings Account (HSA) or an

emergency fund—you can alleviate the burden when unexpected expenses arise.

- **Moving Costs:** Moving can be expensive, yet many consider it an unexpected event. By saving incrementally for moving expenses, you can transition to a new home without scrambling for cash.

- **Rent Increases:** Rent hikes are often inevitable. By monitoring rental trends and saving specifically for these increases, you can absorb the costs without resorting to debt.

Preparation is essential for financial peace. When you can anticipate and plan for life's inevitable disruptions, you reduce both emotional and financial stress. An emergency fund is not just a reactive measure; it's a proactive strategy for navigating life's ups and downs with confidence. By viewing "emergencies" as predictable and manageable, you can transform them into opportunities for demonstrating financial responsibility and resilience.

Building a Savings Habit and Finding Motivation

Saving money, especially in the early stages, can often feel like a daunting task. The results may seem slow to materialize, and the discipline required to remain consistent can feel discouraging. You might glance at the modest amount you manage to set aside each month and question whether it's worth the effort. This common struggle can be overcome with perseverance, small wins, and a shift in your mindset.

The Emotional Challenge of Early-Stage Saving

At the beginning of your savings journey, progress can feel painfully sluggish. It's easy to feel frustrated when you've only managed to save a few hundred dollars over several months while expenses and obligations keep piling up. The emotional challenge often stems from the disconnect between your efforts and the tangible results. This is where many people tend to give up, believing that their minor contributions aren't making a significant impact.

However, it's important to recognize that even small steps count. Financial stability is a marathon, not a sprint. Building wealth and security takes time, but with consistent action, those small savings accumulate—similar to how compound interest works. What may appear insignificant today can lead to substantial changes in the long run, and consistency is key to making progress.

Starting with Small Steps: The Power of Discipline

The most effective way to embark on your savings journey is by focusing on small, manageable changes in your life. It's not about radically altering your lifestyle overnight, but rather making consistent adjustments that add up over time. These changes can be simple, such as:

- **Canceling unnecessary subscriptions:** Review your monthly recurring charges. Are there services you seldom use, like subscriptions to streaming platforms, magazines, or gym memberships? Cutting back on these minor yet consistent expenses can free up additional funds that can be directed into your savings.
- **Reducing unnecessary spending:** Analyze your daily or weekly habits. Perhaps you're spending excessively on takeout meals, impulse buys, or unneeded shopping. By becoming more aware of your spending, you can identify areas to cut back. This doesn't mean depriving yourself entirely; it's about

finding a balance and making intentional choices that align with your financial goals.

These small lifestyle adjustments might seem trivial initially, but they help develop the discipline necessary for building enduring habits. Much like training for a marathon, saving money demands steady effort and consistency. The more you practice these habits, the easier they become, and over time, they'll feel like second nature.

The Natural Hair Color Anecdote: Understanding Trade-Offs

Building savings isn't solely about cutting back on spending; it's also about understanding and embracing trade-offs. This can be particularly challenging when you want to maintain a certain lifestyle but can't afford every expense.

Consider the decision of whether to color your hair. It may seem like a minor, personal choice, but it serves as a metaphor for broader financial decisions. You might feel compelled to keep up with a particular look or trend, but there's a financial reality to consider. Opting for a natural hair color instead of frequent coloring appointments could save a significant amount of money. By making the trade-off to reduce one small expense, you're able to invest that money elsewhere—perhaps into your emergency fund or towards a vacation you truly desire.

This principle extends to larger financial choices as well. Choosing to forgo an extravagant weekend getaway or buy fewer designer clothes may be tough initially, but it's ultimately a decision that yields greater long-term benefits. The ability to make these trade-offs will help you cultivate a robust, sustainable savings habit. Over time, these decisions accumulate, strengthening not only your financial health but also teaching you the value of delayed gratification and mindful spending.

Celebrating Early Wins and Building Momentum

As you progress on your savings journey, it's crucial to acknowledge the small victories along the way. Initially, your savings account may not seem to grow quickly, but every deposit is a step toward a more secure financial future. Celebrating these wins, no matter how small, is essential for maintaining motivation. Whether it's the first time you manage to save $100 or reach your goal of having one month's worth of living expenses in your emergency fund, take the time to celebrate.

These early successes may feel minor, but they are significant milestones on the path to financial security. Take pride in the discipline you are cultivating, and reward yourself in ways that don't undermine your progress. Celebrating could mean treating yourself to a nice dinner (without going overboard), enjoying a relaxing evening, or doing something that acknowledges your hard work without derailing your budget.

Building momentum is vital. The more you observe your savings grow, the more motivated you'll feel to continue making wise financial choices. Over time, your savings will grow to the point where it will no longer feel like a struggle. What once seemed like a daunting task evolves into a routine part of your life, and you'll find yourself naturally inclined to save more as your financial confidence flourishes.

Saving in Different Life Stages and Relationship Dynamics

Saving strategies evolve throughout various life stages, and the approach can significantly differ depending on whether you're navigating life as an individual or as part of a dual-income household. Whether single, married, or in a partnership, understanding how to save efficiently and adapt to life's changes is crucial for maintaining financial stability. Moreover, a solid savings plan can greatly reduce tension in relationships and prepare both individuals and families for life's inevitable transitions.

Saving Strategies: Individuals vs. Dual-Income Households

When you're on your own, saving can sometimes feel like a solitary endeavor, but it offers flexibility. You have full control over your finances, making budgeting and saving easier to manage without needing to coordinate with someone else's financial priorities. However, this independence can also come with challenges—especially if you experience unexpected financial setbacks.

For individuals, the key is creating a savings structure that covers both short-term and long-term needs. This includes:

- Emergency funds: Aim to have at least one month of living expenses in an easily accessible savings account.
- Regular contributions: Set aside a portion of your income each month, even if it's small, for future goals like retirement or a down payment on a home.
- Strategic planning: Utilize automated tools and apps to track spending and savings goals, helping to avoid the temptation to overspend.

In contrast, dual-income households experience a different dynamic. Having two incomes means you can potentially save more, but it also introduces the need for clear financial communication and cooperation. Joint financial goals can include:

- **Pooling resources**: Combine income to meet shared goals, such as saving for a family vacation or home improvement.
- **Separate vs. joint accounts**: Decide whether to maintain individual accounts for personal expenses or have a joint account for shared household costs. Both approaches have pros and cons, but clarity in decision-making is key.
- **Income distribution**: Ensure that both parties contribute fairly to joint savings goals, even if income levels differ, to prevent feelings of financial imbalance.

While dual-income households may have more disposable income, they also need to focus on communication and alignment in their saving strategies. Setting clear expectations about responsibilities—whether managing the household budget or saving for specific goals—can make the saving process smoother.

The Role of Financial Preparedness in Reducing Relationship Tension

Finances are one of the most common sources of stress in relationships. A lack of financial preparedness can lead to arguments, feelings of insecurity, and long-term dissatisfaction. Conversely, couples who actively save together and make financial decisions collaboratively tend to experience less tension and better overall relationship satisfaction.

Saving in a partnership offers significant advantages:

- **Shared goals and accountability**: When both partners work toward the same financial goals, it fosters a sense of teamwork. This is especially important when planning for milestones like buying a home or starting a family.

- **Financial independence within the relationship:** Even in a dual-income household, it's important for both partners to maintain some financial independence. Each person should have savings or investments separate from household funds, reducing feelings of resentment or dependency.

- **Stress reduction in times of crisis:** Having an emergency fund and savings for specific goals can drastically reduce financial stress during challenges. Knowing you have the financial backup to handle situations like job loss or unexpected expenses provides significant relief.

Savings as a Protective Measure for Major Life Transitions

Life is full of transitions and significant changes, such as moving, job loss, starting a business, or becoming a parent, that require financial preparedness. Savings act as a buffer against these inevitable transitions, giving individuals and couples the peace of mind to handle change without compromising their financial stability.

- **Moving:** Relocating for a new job or personal reasons can incur various costs, such as hiring movers and utility deposits. Having a savings cushion can make this process smoother and prevent debt.

- **Job Loss:** Job loss is a major stressor and a common reason for falling back into debt. A well-funded emergency fund is critical, allowing you to maintain stability while searching for a new job.

- **Starting a Business:** Entrepreneurs face significant financial hurdles when launching a new business. A robust savings foundation can provide the runway needed to navigate the tough initial months or years.

- **Parenthood:** Planning for a baby or expanding a family involves various costs, including medical expenses and childcare. Having dedicated savings for this transition helps offset these costs, ensuring you're not financially strained during this time.

Strategic Saving and Opportunity Readiness

While retirement accounts like 401(k)s and IRAs are crucial for long-term financial security, it's essential to maintain a balance between these long-term savings and short- to medium-term funds that offer access and flexibility. Strategic saving involves setting aside funds that are readily available for opportunities and emergencies, ensuring you are financially agile when the right moment arises.

The Importance of Access and Liquidity

Liquidity refers to how easily and quickly you can access your money without incurring significant penalties or losing value. Although retirement accounts provide tax benefits, they are designed for long-term growth and often come with restrictions, such as age requirements or early withdrawal penalties. While these restrictions are suitable for long-term goals, they can hinder your ability to respond to short-term needs or unexpected opportunities.

For instance, you might find yourself in a position where you need funds for a business investment, a down payment on a home, or an unexpected educational opportunity. In such cases, having liquid assets—funds that can be accessed easily without tax burdens—becomes invaluable. Saving for specific goals outside of retirement accounts allows you to capitalize on opportunities without waiting years to access your funds.

The Opportunity Cost of Tying Up All Assets in Retirement Accounts

One key financial principle is opportunity cost, which refers to the value of the opportunities you forego when making one financial decision over another. While saving for the future in retirement accounts is important, you may miss out on valuable opportunities in the present if all your savings are tied up.

For example, if all your savings are in retirement accounts, you might find it challenging to:

- **Invest in a House:** A home can be an excellent investment, but you need accessible funds for a down payment and closing costs. If your savings are locked away in retirement funds, you may miss the chance to purchase a home or face delays accessing those funds.

- **Launch a Business:** Starting a business often requires significant upfront investment. If your savings are solely in retirement accounts, you might have to take on debt or delay your entrepreneurial goals while waiting for your retirement funds to grow.

- **Retire Early:** If your retirement accounts are your only savings, transitioning to an early retirement or pursuing new passions may be financially restrictive. Having savings outside retirement accounts allows for greater flexibility without penalties.

The key takeaway is that while retirement accounts are vital for long-term wealth-building, they shouldn't be your only savings vehicle. Balancing long-term and short-term savings is crucial for maintaining financial flexibility.

Encouraging After-Tax Investing for Greater Financial Flexibility

After-tax investments refer to money invested in taxable accounts, which are not bound by the same restrictions as retirement accounts. While these funds don't offer the immediate tax advantages of retirement savings, they provide accessibility and liquidity when opportunities arise.

Here are some reasons why after-tax investing is essential for strategic saving:

- **Accessibility:** Taxable brokerage accounts allow you to buy and sell investments without the constraints of retirement account rules. You can withdraw funds as needed without penalties, providing greater liquidity.
- **Investment Flexibility:** Taxable accounts enable you to invest in various assets, such as stocks, bonds, and real estate, allowing you to tailor investments based on your goals.
- **Tax Efficiency:** While taxable accounts don't provide tax-deferred growth, effective tax strategies can reduce your tax burden, like utilizing tax-loss harvesting or holding investments for the long term to benefit from lower capital gains rates.

Encouraging after-tax investments doesn't mean disregarding retirement accounts; it simply means incorporating both types of savings into your financial plan to balance long-term wealth-building with short-term flexibility.

The Value of Having Money That's "Ready to Deploy"

One of the most powerful aspects of strategic saving is having money that's "ready to deploy" when opportunities arise. Whether it's purchasing property, seizing a business opportunity, or investing in something aligned with your long-term goals, having cash or easily liquidated investments allows you to act promptly.

Opportunities often appear unexpectedly, and without ready access to capital, you might miss out. For instance, an investment opportunity may require a quick decision and a timely deposit. If all your funds are tied up in retirement accounts, you may have to miss the opportunity or incur expensive loans. Maintaining a portion of your savings in liquid accounts enhances your financial agility.

Additionally, life is full of moments where access to funds can profoundly impact your situation. Whether helping a family member in need or investing in a personal passion, the ability to deploy savings as needed adds freedom and empowerment, significantly enhancing your financial and personal life.

The essence of strategic saving is understanding the balance between preparing for the future and having the flexibility to act in the present. Whether you're saving for retirement, a down payment on a house, or a major business venture, your approach should prioritize both accessibility and long-term growth.

The Discipline of Delayed Gratification

The concept of delayed gratification is a fundamental principle for achieving financial success. It involves resisting the lure of immediate rewards in favor of long-term benefits. This principle not only plays a vital role in saving money but also serves as a cornerstone for success in various life areas, including business, personal development, and the fulfillment of long-term goals. Cultivating the discipline to delay gratification empowers you to remain focused on your financial and life objectives, especially when achieving them requires sacrifices and self-control.

Long-Term Rewards of Patience and Discipline

At its essence, delayed gratification is about understanding that today's efforts will yield future rewards. For savers, this often means forgoing short-term pleasures—such as dining out regularly, purchasing the latest gadgets, or spending on unnecessary luxuries—to build a financial cushion for tomorrow. While the benefits of this discipline may not be immediate, over time, it transforms into financial stability, growth opportunities, and the freedom to make choices without the constant burden of financial insecurity.

The rewards of delayed gratification can feel intangible at first. It may be frustrating to watch friends or colleagues indulge in a more lavish lifestyle while you prioritize saving for the future. However, as months and years pass, your savings will accumulate, and your financial foundation will strengthen. Ultimately, your patience will lead to long-term security, the ability to make significant investments, and the comfort of knowing you have resources to handle life's unexpected challenges.

For instance, saving for retirement might require sacrificing a higher salary today to contribute to a 401(k) or other retirement plans. It could also mean limiting impulse spending to fund an emergency savings account that protects you during unexpected job loss or health crises. The beauty of delayed gratification lies in its capacity to secure the life you desire in the future while enabling conscious and responsible present-day choices.

Delayed Gratification: A Foundational Trait for Success in Business and Life

The practice of delayed gratification extends beyond saving money; it's a vital mindset for success across various life domains. In business, entrepreneurship, and personal growth, the ability to delay gratification distinguishes those who persevere through challenges from those who seek immediate results. Building a business, mastering a skill, or achieving significant personal goals necessitates the discipline to endure early difficulties and persist despite temporary setbacks.

Consider an entrepreneur launching a new venture: initial success may be slow, and returns on investments of time and money might not be immediately visible. While it's tempting to seek quick results and take shortcuts, thriving businesses are built on patience, hard work, and a steadfast commitment to long-term goals. In this context, delayed gratification refers to investing resources without expecting immediate profit, trusting that rewards will materialize as the business develops.

Similarly, for anyone pursuing personal growth—whether advancing in their career, learning new skills, or improving their health—delayed gratification is essential. Results from consistent effort—such as daily workouts, continuous learning, or overcoming challenges—often don't manifest immediately, but they compound over time. The ability to delay gratification and maintain focus on long-term goals is a key trait that enables sustained success and personal fulfillment.

Mindset Shift: "If it were easy, everyone would do it."

Developing the discipline of delayed gratification requires a significant mindset shift, one that contrasts sharply with the instant gratification culture prevalent today. The desire for immediate rewards is natural and deeply ingrained in human behavior, but those who achieve financial success recognize that lasting wealth and stability demand perseverance and restraint.

The phrase "If it were easy, everyone would do it" encapsulates this mindset shift. Financial success, especially regarding savings, is not about following the crowd or opting for the easiest path. It involves doing the hard work today, even when uncomfortable, to secure a brighter future tomorrow. True financial freedom comes from making short-term sacrifices that lead to greater long-term stability.

This shift in mindset is crucial when facing the hurdles of saving money, paying off debt, or investing in long-term goals. It's easy to succumb to the pressure to spend, follow trends, or indulge in temporary pleasures. However, embracing the understanding that financial success requires dedication and sacrifices ultimately distinguishes those who succeed from those who don't.

Building the Habit of Delayed Gratification

Establishing the habit of delayed gratification doesn't happen overnight. It requires consistent practice and a conscious decision to prioritize long-term goals over immediate desires. Creating a system that facilitates adherence to this discipline is key.

Here are some strategies for cultivating this habit:

- **Set Clear, Tangible Goals:** Clearly define what you're saving for—be it an emergency fund, a house down payment, or retirement—making it easier to stay focused and motivated.

Regularly remind yourself of the benefits associated with achieving these goals.

- **Automate Savings:** Establish automatic transfers from your checking account to savings or investment accounts. This approach removes the temptation to spend the money and transforms saving into a consistent habit.
- **Track Progress:** Monitor your advancement toward your goals. Celebrating small milestones can build momentum and reinforce the value of delayed gratification.
- **Avoid Impulsive Spending Triggers:** Identify situations or environments that lead to impulsive spending and create strategies to avoid them, such as unsubscribing from marketing emails or steering clear of stores that tempt you to buy unnecessary items.
- **Practice Small Sacrifices:** Start by delaying gratification in minor ways, like skipping a morning coffee or reducing entertainment expenses, gradually working up to larger financial objectives.

Balancing Risk and Reward in the Saver's World

Savers are often characterized by their cautious approach to finances, which emphasizes security and stability. This mindset typically leads to a strong aversion to market risk, driven by a fear of losing hard-earned money. However, to build a well-rounded financial strategy, it is essential to find a thoughtful balance between risk and reward. In this section, we will explore how savers can gradually embrace risk in a manner that aligns with their long-term goals, utilizing principles of diversification, strategic investing, and an understanding of market behavior.

The Cautious Nature of Savers and Aversion to Market Risk

Savers generally steer clear of risk, particularly in volatile markets. Their primary focus is on wealth preservation rather than rapid growth, which often leads them to rely heavily on low-risk, low-return investments such as savings accounts or certificates of deposit (CDs). While these options offer safety, they typically do not provide the necessary growth to accumulate significant wealth over time.

For savers conditioned to view risk as a threat, the idea of investing in the stock market or other higher-risk ventures can feel daunting. Media narratives about market crashes and financial losses can intensify these fears, causing many savers to avoid the stock market entirely, even when it could offer better returns.

However, it is crucial for savers to recognize that completely avoiding risk may hinder their ability to achieve financial goals, such as purchasing a home, funding education, or enjoying a comfortable retirement. While market risks are indeed real, they can be managed through strategic planning and diversified investing.

Gradually Becoming Comfortable with Calculated Risk

To help savers grow comfortable with risk, the concept of calculated risk is essential—this involves carefully evaluating potential rewards while managing the likelihood of losses. This approach allows savers to dip their toes into investing while still safeguarding their financial future.

A practical starting point for savers is to invest in low-cost mutual funds and exchange-traded funds (ETFs), which provide built-in diversification. These investment vehicles enable individuals to pool their money with other investors to acquire a wide range of securities, such as stocks, bonds, or commodities. By diversifying their investments across multiple assets, savers can reduce the impact of any single investment on their overall portfolio.

Savers should aim for diversified portfolios that include a mix of asset classes—such as stocks, bonds, and real estate investment trusts (REITs)—to spread risk across different sectors. Target-date funds are another appealing option, as they automatically adjust asset allocation based on the investor's timeline and risk tolerance. This structured approach is especially beneficial for savers new to investing, allowing them to gradually increase risk exposure as they move closer to their financial goals.

Overcoming the Fear of Loss Through Education and Long-Term Market Trends

The fear of loss is one of the most significant barriers preventing savers from embracing calculated risk. Many savers become so fixated on avoiding downturns that they overlook the long-term growth potential of the market. Short-term market fluctuations can trigger panic or anxiety when investments dip, making it challenging to stay the course.

However, understanding long-term growth trends can help alleviate these fears. Historically, stock markets have demonstrated resilience, recovering from downturns and offering substantial growth potential to long-term investors. For instance, the S&P 500, which tracks 500 of the largest companies in the United States, has historically produced an average annual return of around 7% to 10% after inflation over extended periods. This steady growth can significantly surpass the returns of savings accounts or bonds over time.

Educating oneself about market cycles—acknowledging that downturns are natural and often temporary—can reduce the fear of loss. Savers who understand economic cycles (including recessions, bull markets, and bear markets) and how to navigate market volatility are better equipped to remain calm during temporary setbacks. The goal is not to avoid risk entirely but to manage it wisely.

It's also beneficial for savers to consider historical performance when assessing risk. A well-diversified and strategically managed investment portfolio allows savers to weather short-term losses with greater ease. When framed within the context of long-term gains, the fear of loss becomes less daunting.

Balancing Risk and Reward: A Continuous Process

Balancing risk and reward is not a one-time decision; it requires ongoing reassessment and adjustment based on personal circumstances, market conditions, and life goals. Savers should feel empowered to revisit their portfolios and modify their risk exposure as they gain experience or as their life situations evolve.

As their financial situations improve or their comfort with risk grows, savers can gradually incorporate more high-risk, high-reward investments into their portfolios, such as individual stocks or alternative investments. Conversely, if their financial goals change or they approach a life stage that necessitates greater security (like nearing retirement), they may opt to reduce exposure to riskier investments and pivot toward more conservative options.

Conclusion: Saving as Empowerment

As we wrap up our exploration of the art and discipline of saving, it's essential to recognize the profound benefits that saving offers. Saving money is not merely a practical act; it is a powerful tool of empowerment. It enables wealth building while fostering confidence, peace of mind, and a sense of freedom that spending alone cannot provide.

Building Confidence and Peace of Mind

The transformative power of saving is undeniable. Every dollar saved, every emergency fund established, and every investment made contributes to your self-assurance and financial security. Being prepared for life's unexpected challenges—be it a surprise car repair, medical bills, or job loss—instills control over your circumstances. This control enhances your mental well-being, reducing stress and anxiety related to financial uncertainty.

While external factors like economic shifts or unexpected crises can shake our sense of security, a solid saving strategy provides a stable foundation that can withstand many challenges. No longer must you live in fear of the unknown; you can face life's uncertainties with greater confidence, resilience, and peace of mind.

This financial autonomy is particularly empowering for those who have felt constrained by their financial situation in the past. With each small deposit, you create a security net that supports not just your material needs but also your emotional well-being. Financial stability fosters peace of mind, which is invaluable in our often unpredictable world.

Reducing Life Stress and Strengthening Relationships

Beyond individual confidence, savings significantly alleviate the stress that financial instability can impose on relationships. Financial difficulties are frequently cited as a leading cause of conflict in romantic partnerships, family dynamics, and friendships. When money is tight, every financial decision becomes charged with tension, leading to frustration and emotional exhaustion.

Having a well-established savings plan can dramatically ease these pressures, allowing for open communication and collaboration. Partners can tackle life's challenges together without the constant anxiety of resource scarcity. Families can focus on long-term goals rather than being mired in immediate financial needs. Savings empower both individuals and couples to make thoughtful, less-stressful decisions, enhancing their relationships.

Moreover, financial stability opens up opportunities for vacations, home improvements, educational pursuits, and investing in shared dreams. These possibilities, often unattainable without solid savings, become part of a long-term vision that nurtures personal growth and familial bonds.

Creating Room for Future Opportunities

One of the most compelling aspects of saving is the optional freedom it provides. Saving not only prepares you for emergencies but also creates avenues for new possibilities. Whether it's starting a business, returning to school, or taking a sabbatical to explore, having savings gives you the luxury of choice. You can pursue passions and take calculated risks without the overhang of financial failure.

Additionally, savings provide the leverage to capitalize on opportunities that may not be available if you're living paycheck to paycheck. Want to invest in a promising venture? Having liquid funds allows you to act when the time is right. Dreaming of early retirement? The more you save now, the sooner you can design the life you envision.

In essence, the freedom that comes from saving empowers you to make decisions aligned with your values and aspirations, rather than being driven by external pressures or financial constraints.

Staying the Course: The Long Game

While the benefits of saving are clear, the journey to financial security is often neither quick nor easy. It requires patience, discipline, and consistency—qualities that can feel challenging to uphold in a culture that often prizes instant gratification. Remember, financial security is a marathon, not a sprint.

It's easy to feel discouraged when progress seems slow, especially in the early stages of saving. You might think your small contributions don't amount to much. However, over time, these small actions will snowball into something significant. Whether through the power of compound interest or the security provided by having a safety net, consistent saving will yield dividends in the long run.

When you feel like progress is slow, take a moment to reflect on how far you've come. Each deposit into your savings is another building block in your path to financial freedom. Trust the process, believe in the cumulative power of your efforts, and recognize that the sacrifices you make today lay the groundwork for the life you desire tomorrow.

Ultimately, saving transcends being a mere financial strategy—it embodies a mindset that empowers you to take control of your life, reduce stress, and craft the future you envision. By building savings, you gain confidence, peace of mind, and the ability to seize opportunities that resonate with your goals. Saving is not about deprivation; it's about empowerment. It's about creating space to live intentionally, make choices that reflect your values, and navigate life's challenges with grace and stability.

Chapter Six: Growth Mindset: Cultivating Wealth

The Shift from Saver to Grower Mindset

I once had the opportunity to work with a high-net-worth client who, despite earning a significant income, felt trapped—both emotionally and mentally—by his job. He described his daily routine as not only exhausting but also hopeless, caught in a cycle that seemed impossible to escape. Although he chased money relentlessly, it never provided the freedom or fulfillment he truly desired.

The pivotal moment came when we redefined his perspective on money. Instead of viewing his work merely as a means to survive or pay bills, he began to see it as a choice—a powerful one. I shared with him, "You work because you choose to, not because you have to." This shift in mindset was transformative, ushering in what I refer to as the "grower" mentality.

This transformation went beyond mere numbers or investments; it represented an emotional and psychological breakthrough. He started to perceive money as a tool for freedom and growth, rather than a burden or source of stress. This newfound perspective granted him control over his life and future in ways that simply saving never could.

As an advisor, moments like these are profoundly rewarding for me. Guiding clients beyond the confines of scarcity and fear to embrace abundance and strategic growth is at the heart of my work. It's not solely about managing wealth; it's about revolutionizing how individuals relate to money itself.

Grower

A grower is someone who transcends the basic principles of saving and prioritizing security. Rather than merely accumulating wealth and safeguarding what they possess, a grower actively seeks out strategic growth opportunities to achieve higher returns. This shift in mindset embraces the belief that money can—and should—work harder to build lasting wealth.

At the core of being a grower is a willingness to accept calculated risks. Unlike savers, who often concentrate on avoiding losses at all costs, growers recognize that risk is an inevitable and essential component of the journey. They perceive risk not as a source of fear but as a valuable tool that can lead to gains when markets and opportunities align favorably.

This perspective requires a nuanced understanding of volatility. Growers focus on positioning themselves to capitalize on prosperous years, fully aware that downturns are both temporary and manageable with a well-thought-out strategy. They refuse to allow the fear of short-term losses to dictate their long-term financial approach.

Crucially, the transition from saver to grower is a deeply personal journey. The definition of "enough money" varies for each individual—whether it's sufficient to cover basic needs, support a family, or provide the freedom to pursue passions. Once this threshold is crossed, the focus naturally shifts from protection to growth. It becomes about making money work smarter, not just harder.

The Role of Tax Strategy in the Grower Mindset

For growers, the focus extends beyond merely pursuing higher returns; it also involves strategic thinking around taxes. While taxes can often feel like a "necessary evil" that hinders wealth accumulation, savvy growers understand that they don't have to be a fixed cost. With careful planning, taxes can be managed, minimized, and even leveraged to enhance overall financial outcomes.

Consider a client who was facing an annual tax bill exceeding $100,000 on their investment income. Through a combination of tax-efficient investment vehicles, strategic asset location, and timing of income recognition, we successfully reduced their tax burden to just $7,000—without compromising their take-home pay or lifestyle.

This approach to tax-aware investing does more than just improve the numbers on paper; it significantly alters the retirement income outlook and boosts financial confidence. When clients witness the impact that a well-crafted tax strategy can have—allowing them to retain more of their earnings while still pursuing growth—they begin to feel empowered rather than constrained by their financial decisions.

Real-Life Client Examples of Grower Strategies

Let's consider a couple from California earning a combined $300,000 in W-2 income. They are hardworking professionals and disciplined savers, yet they felt overwhelmed by their tax burden and the impending cost of college tuition. Like many high-income families, they were doing everything "right"—maxing out their 401(k)s, saving for college, and avoiding unnecessary debt—but still watched a significant portion of their income vanish to taxes.

We introduced a strategic investment that effectively reduced their taxable income by $90,000. As a result, they received a $30,000 tax refund, which they immediately allocated toward their child's college tuition. The impact of this change was not just financial; it was profoundly emotional. For the first time, they felt as if the system was working in their favor. They weren't just laboring for money—now their money was actively working for them.

These victories create lasting shifts in how clients perceive their finances. Initially, many clients are hesitant; the transition from a conservative saver to a strategic grower can feel uncomfortable, sometimes even risky. However, through transparency, education, and by sharing personal experiences and similar success stories, trust is established. And with that trust comes transformation.

I still recall the phone calls after that first tax season. "We just got our refund—$30,000! We thought you were exaggerating." These moments are significant. They're not just confirmations of strategy; they represent liberation for families who have long felt trapped in a high-earning, high-tax cycle.

Understanding Different Tax Types and Their Impact on Investments

Not all income is taxed equally, and this fundamental truth can dramatically reshape an individual's financial strategy. One of the first breakthroughs many growers encounter is understanding the hierarchy of tax efficiency.

At the top of the "worst tax" list is W-2 income. This includes your salary or hourly wage—earned income subjected to the full weight of the tax system: federal income tax, state income tax, Social Security, and Medicare. For high earners, this can result in losing 40% or more of every dollar earned to taxes.

Next in line are retirement distributions from pre-tax accounts like 401(k)s or traditional IRAs. These amounts are taxed as ordinary income, often placing retirees back into higher tax brackets—especially if they've successfully saved and invested over the years. The irony here is that achieving financial success can lead to paying more in retirement than anticipated.

In contrast, capital gains—especially long-term capital gains—enjoy more favorable tax treatment. When you hold an investment for over a year, the gains are typically taxed at 15% or 20% (plus a potential 3.8% net investment income tax for high earners), which is substantially lower than ordinary income rates. Even better, some qualified dividends fall under this same advantageous tax treatment.

But what's the ultimate goal? Tax-free income. Whether it comes from a properly structured Roth IRA, municipal bonds, or strategic use of life insurance, tax-free income in retirement not only reduces your tax burden but can also help preserve Social Security benefits and lower Medicare premiums.

Let's compare:

- A client earning $200,000 in W-2 income might owe $60,000 or more in combined taxes.
- A client realizing $200,000 in long-term capital gains might owe less than $40,000—and with smart planning, potentially even less.

That's a $20,000+ difference in taxes for the same amount of income. If that income can be structured to be partially or fully tax-free, the savings can soar even higher.

This is why growers don't simply ask, "How much am I earning?"—they delve deeper, asking, "What kind of income am I earning, and how is it taxed?" The answers to these questions can mean the difference between merely scraping by and truly thriving in retirement.

The Importance of Tax Awareness for Growers

For growers, achieving financial success goes beyond merely earning more—it's about keeping more. This necessitates not only wise investing but also a profound understanding of how taxes influence every financial decision. Tax awareness is a fundamental pillar of the grower mindset, enabling investors to build wealth more efficiently and sustainably.

Strategic Tools for Tax-Efficient Investing

Growers recognize that the structure of their investments can be just as critical as the returns themselves. Tools such as tax-loss harvesting, depreciation, and capital gains management are essential components of the grower's toolkit.

Tax-loss harvesting is a prime example. By selling investments that have declined in value and immediately reinvesting in similar assets (while adhering to wash sale rules), investors can offset taxable gains elsewhere in their portfolio. This strategy maintains market exposure while effectively reducing the tax burden.

Depreciation serves as another powerful tool, particularly for those involved in real estate or business ventures. Growers who hold rental properties, for instance, can utilize depreciation to shelter income, thereby lowering their tax liability without affecting cash flow.

Moreover, capital gains can be meticulously managed—strategically selling investments to remain within lower tax brackets or spacing out gains over time to avoid triggering higher marginal rates.

Mutual Funds vs. Tax-Efficient Alternatives

A surprising revelation for many new growers is the hidden tax cost associated with mutual funds. Mutual fund investors can face capital gains distributions—even if they haven't sold any shares—due to the fund itself selling appreciated assets. These distributions can lead to unexpected tax bills, even in losing years.

In contrast, ETFs and individually managed stocks offer enhanced tax control. ETFs, with their "in-kind" redemption structure, tend to be more tax-efficient and rarely distribute capital gains. Individual stocks provide even greater control, allowing investors to decide when to realize gains or losses, facilitating tax opportunities, and minimizing unexpected surprises.

Tax Strategy as Risk Management

While many associate risk with market volatility or asset allocation, tax risk is equally significant—and often overlooked. Poor diversification can adversely affect returns and lead to unnecessary taxes. For example, an overconcentration in a single stock may limit tax-loss opportunities, while excessive reliance on pre-tax retirement accounts can result in soaring required minimum distributions (RMDs) later in life, unexpectedly pushing retirees into higher tax brackets.

Growers leverage tax strategy as a form of risk management—smoothing income, minimizing potential tax spikes, and enhancing after-tax returns. It's not solely about today's tax implications, but about creating a sustainable and efficient income stream for the future.

Wash Sale Rules: A Crucial Detail

When engaging in tax-loss harvesting, growers must be particularly attentive to wash-sale rules. These IRS regulations disallow the deduction of a loss if the same or a "substantially identical" investment is repurchased within 30 days before or after the sale. Violating these rules can negate the loss and lead to penalties or confusion during tax season.

That's why growers and their advisors carefully monitor transaction timing and utilize alternatives (such as sector ETFs or similar stocks) to maintain market exposure without violating IRS regulations.

The Advisor's Role in Educating and Guiding Growers

One of the most vital relationships for individuals transitioning to the grower mindset is with their advisor. However, many advisors—particularly those entrenched in traditional models—tend to focus exclusively on saving strategies and risk minimization. While these factors are important, they often overlook one of the most significant levers in a grower's toolbox: taxes.

Beyond Risk and Return: The Tax Conversation

Too often, advisors treat tax planning as "someone else's job." They may optimize portfolios for growth or protection, but rarely take the time to grasp the client's complete tax picture. For growers, the distinction between an effective tax strategy and a passive one can translate into tens or even hundreds of thousands of dollars in savings over a lifetime.

The best advisors go beyond generic advice. They conduct annual reviews of tax returns, collaborate with CPAs, and assist clients in understanding the relationship between tax strategy and investment choices. This proactive approach ensures that investments are not only working hard but are also working smart—aligned with the client's tax situation, long-term goals, and risk tolerance.

Real-World Examples: When Advisors Step In

I recall a client whose tax preparer dismissed the tax benefits of a real estate syndication investment, stating, "These losses won't help you." The client, feeling confused and concerned, nearly walked away from an opportunity that was perfectly suited to him. Upon further review, we discovered that the preparer had misclassified the investment on the return, disqualifying losses that could have significantly offset other income. Once corrected, the client's tax liability dropped by over $40,000.

In another instance, a client's CPA advised against Roth conversions during a temporary dip in income, reasoning, "Why pay taxes now if you can delay?" However, a broader analysis revealed a clear opportunity: converting to a Roth at a low marginal rate would substantially reduce future required minimum distributions (RMDs) and enhance long-term retirement flexibility. When presented with the full impact through tax projections, the client proceeded with confidence.

These examples are not isolated incidents; they are quite common. They underscore why tax professionals, while essential, often adopt an overly conservative approach. Their primary role is typically to report history rather than shape the future. A forward-thinking advisor bridges this gap, helping clients evaluate short-term costs against long-term benefits.

Balance Is Key: Growth and Prudence

Of course, tax planning alone isn't sufficient. Some clients may work with CPAs who are exceptional tax strategists but overly cautious when it comes to investing. These professionals are trained to avoid mistakes and prevent surprises—not necessarily to pursue opportunities. This is where a skilled advisor can find the right balance, understanding risk, growth, and tax impact simultaneously.

An ideal advisor for a grower isn't merely a numbers person. They act as a translator, simplifying complex tax and investment strategies into clear decisions. They are also a teacher, empowering clients with knowledge rather than simply selling products. Above all, they serve as a guide, leading with foresight and flexibility instead of rigid rules.

Personal Reflections on Growth and Experience

In the early years of my career, like many in the financial industry, my focus was quite narrow: help clients grow their assets and generate returns. The core pillars of my practice revolved around income generation, portfolio allocation, and risk mitigation. Taxes? That was strictly the domain of the CPA.

However, as I began working with more affluent clients—particularly those transitioning from savers to growers—I realized that wealth isn't solely about what you make; it's significantly about what you keep. And what you keep is often determined not by market performance, but by the IRS.

This insight didn't come to me overnight. It developed through countless meetings where clients expressed sentiments such as, "I made good money last year, but I don't feel like I'm getting ahead," or "I'm working harder than ever, and my tax bill keeps climbing." I started to ask deeper questions, review tax returns, study the tax code, and collaborate with CPAs. Over time, I came to appreciate the profound synergy between investment strategy and tax strategy—a synergy that too many advisors overlook.

When Tax Strategy Meets Investment Insight

The most successful outcomes I've witnessed haven't stemmed from simply outperforming the market; they've emerged from outsmarting the system—legally and ethically. This involves optimizing asset location, harvesting losses, leveraging depreciation, and selecting investments not just for their growth potential but for their after-tax returns.

This shift in perspective transformed my practice—and my clients' lives. I began forging deeper relationships with tax professionals, not merely to execute a plan but to co-create one. I learned to communicate in their language and became the connector between a client's investment vision and their tax reality. When that triangle—client, advisor, and tax expert—operates in harmony, the results are far more significant than any individual component.

The Power of Your Circle

Perhaps the most personal evolution I experienced was recognizing the importance of my surroundings. I began to spend more time with peers who were financially sophisticated, intellectually curious, and strategically driven. These weren't just individuals who made money—they were people who understood how to think about money.

Being in those environments transformed me. It challenged me to elevate my own thinking. I wasn't just learning strategies; I was adopting mindsets. That's when I truly embraced the role of a "grower" in my own life. I started applying the same strategies I recommended to my clients to my personal finances, and I began to see how my environment—my peer group, my advisors, my education—directly influences my wealth trajectory.

From Advisor to Steward

This transformation has been incredibly rewarding. I no longer view my role as merely that of a financial advisor; I see it as that of a financial steward. I help clients not only grow their wealth but also cultivate confidence, clarity, and control over their financial futures.

Encouragement for Readers: How to Become a Grower

Becoming a grower isn't about chasing high-risk gambles or blindly following market trends. It's about embracing complexity—recognizing that true growth necessitates thoughtful planning, a willingness to ask challenging questions, and a commitment to continuous learning.

Ask the Right Questions

Begin by engaging in a candid conversation with your current financial advisor. Do they request your tax returns? Do they understand how your tax situation impacts your investments? If the answer is no or uncertain, it may be time to seek out someone who will. The ideal advisor doesn't merely discuss returns and risk; they seamlessly integrate tax strategy into every recommendation.

Look for a Balanced Partner

A grower's advisor strikes a balance among three critical elements: growth potential, tax efficiency, and risk management. This equilibrium helps safeguard your capital during downturns while positioning you to seize gains—and tax benefits—when markets rise. Remember, risk isn't solely about avoiding losses; it's about recognizing when calculated risks can result in greater, smarter rewards.

Own Your Financial Education

The grower mindset is fundamentally about empowerment. Commit to learning—not just about investments, but also about taxes, strategies, and how money works for you. Read books, attend seminars, ask your advisor for clarifications, and seek out mentors who encourage you to think differently.

The Grower Mindset as a Path to Financial Freedom

At its essence, the grower mindset represents a profound transformation—from feeling constrained by money to actively choosing how it works for you. It transcends the mere act of saving, focusing instead on strategically growing your wealth in alignment with your values, goals, and lifestyle.

In this mindset, taxes are no longer seen as an unavoidable burden but as a vital component that can be managed and optimized. Risk shifts from being a term to fear to a calculated aspect of growth that, when understood and effectively managed, unlocks new opportunities. Investment strategy evolves to encompass not only returns but also the creation of a sustainable, tax-efficient portfolio that adapts to life's inevitable changes.

The journey toward becoming a grower requires curiosity, courage, and a commitment to lifelong learning. It challenges outdated beliefs about money—such as "saving is enough" or "risk equates to loss"—and replaces them with a mindset that seeks empowerment through knowledge and action.

Financial freedom is not merely about accumulating wealth; it's about having the liberty to live life on your own terms. The grower mindset opens that door, inviting you to step into a future where you work because you choose to, where your money grows intentionally, and where your financial decisions propel the life you envision.

Chapter Seven: Builders: Visionaries Who Shape The World

There are some people in life who appear to operate on another level. They don't just gather riches; they make it, grow it, and then reinvest it in new initiatives, constantly influencing and reshaping their part of the globe. These are the people I've come to refer to as "builders"—serial entrepreneurs, tireless inventors, and visionaries who see chances where others see impediments and, through a unique combination of strategic thinking and sheer drive, make those opportunities a reality.

For years, I identified four primary mindsets when it came to money. But as I rode bikes one day with a friend who had just sold his successful business for a considerable sum, discussing what he was doing next, it dawned on me. There was a rare fifth kind of person, a distinct archetype: the builder. While there might even be a sixth, it's this fifth category that truly stands apart. My friend, instead of simply investing his newfound wealth in traditional ways, was already immersed in starting another company, consulting on new projects, and perpetually exploring avenues to generate more wealth. This wasn't just about making money; it was about the act of creation itself.

The Elusive "Aha!" Moment: From Saver to Builder

When I think about my client's financial experiences, one question constantly arises: at what point does someone shift from a "saver" to a "grower" and then to a "builder"? Many people expect a single, dramatic "light bulb" moment—a rapid flash of understanding that changes their financial outlook. But in my experience, that's rarely how it works. There isn't a magical instant when someone declares, "Aha! I know exactly what I want to do with my money now!" It's far more subtle, a gradual evolution that unfolds over time.

This transition, I've found, is generally tied to how comfortable individuals feel about the amount of money they have invested. That number, of course, is profoundly personal and varies wildly from one person to another. A single man might have a completely different comfort threshold than a single mother. Similarly, a married couple nearing retirement, if they don't feel they have enough saved, will naturally be more conservative and more wary of risk. Conversely, someone who has accumulated a substantial amount of money often develops a profile where they feel, "Yes, I can be a grower because I have enough to withstand the fluctuations that come with growing my wealth."

Interestingly, for many, if there is an "aha!" moment, it often comes during a conversation with a financial advisor about taxes, not in terms of preparing tax returns or finding deductions, but in understanding how to strategically position their money for a better after-tax return. This is where the double-edged sword of success often reveals itself: the more money you make, the more taxes you pay.

People want to make more money, but they certainly don't want to hand over a larger slice to the taxman. This creates a catch-22.

The true revelation for many growers and a foundational understanding for builders comes from grasping the hierarchy of taxation. I've often said this, and it bears repeating: the worst kind of taxation is on W2 income. The second worst is retirement income. The best is tax-free income. But the second best, and incredibly powerful for wealth accumulation, is long-term capital gain. When I sit down with clients and show them the tangible difference in the amount of tax they pay on long-term capital gains versus, say, their W2 or retirement income, something clicks. That's often the moment someone truly embraces the "grower" mindset, and it's a critical step on the path to becoming a builder. It's about the taxation, yes, but more so about optimizing their wealth, which frees up capital and mental energy for building.

The Genesis of a Builder

So, what exactly defines this rare breed, the builder? As I mentioned, they are essentially serial entrepreneurs. They are people who founded their own enterprises, grew and extended them, and then, rather than resting on their laurels, embarked on the next project. This is more than just managing assets; it is about actively creating and adding value.

If a builder came to me and asked me to simply invest all their money, I certainly could. But they inherently know that their greatest value, their quickest path to generating more wealth and control, lies in starting and growing another business.

I haven't encountered many true builders in my career, but those I have met are distinct. I might manage a portion of their money as a "grower," helping them optimize their existing capital, but for the most part, their wealth goes right back into another business, another project, another endeavor to make them even more money. It's a fundamental drive to build, innovate, create something new, or improve upon something existing.

You might think of the archetypal tech entrepreneur who makes a fortune quickly. While impressive, I'd argue that often, these rapid successes involve significant venture capital and a network of seasoned individuals who have "been there and done that." For most builders, the path to mastery, to truly understand how to navigate business entities, legal structures, and taxation, is a journey. It doesn't happen overnight. It's a continuous learning curve, a deep dive into the intricacies of S corps, LLCs, C corps, sole proprietorships, understanding partners, shareholders, and investment capital. These are all crucial pieces of the puzzle for anyone aspiring to build on a grand scale.

I've been fortunate enough to experience a taste of this myself. I've owned my own business for a long time, and I've started other ventures while continually exploring new opportunities that are close enough to my core competencies. Whether you admire him or not, a prime example of this relentless building drive is Elon Musk.

He operates five incredibly diverse businesses—electric cars, robots, rockets, tunnel boring machines, and even brain implants. While his range is extraordinary and not "normal" for most, it perfectly illustrates the builder's instinct: a constant push to create, innovate, and expand. Most builders will, like my friend who sold his business and started another similar one, stick to what's familiar and where their experience lies. This familiarity breeds confidence and expedites the building process.

The Art of Scaling: Beyond the "Do"

If you're out there thinking, "Oh my gosh, I want to start my own business and become a builder," understand that for most people, this takes time and dedication. To accelerate the process, listen to those who have already succeeded. Learn as much as you can about taxes, the legal frameworks around business, and different entity structures. Crucially, surround yourself with other business owners.

And don't be afraid to "trade up" your mentors. If you reach a point where a mentor's tutelage is no longer valuable, it's a sign that you've grown, and it's time to seek out someone who can help you reach the next level. You must keep growing, always.

While I can certainly offer insights for the rare builder, my primary focus in my advisory work is with "growers"—those who are looking to grow their money, preferably with less taxes in mind. However, the lessons from builders are universally applicable. Builders, in my experience, are often the easiest clients to work with because they possess an inherent understanding of risk. They are in business for themselves, and they are generally willing to take calculated risks. Of course, they might earmark some funds as "safe money," and that's entirely fine. But their empire-building approach means we, as advisors, serve as one component in their total financial makeup.

One critical distinction I want to make is that simply owning a business does not automatically make you a builder. There are countless successful business owners who do quite well for themselves. But they often get stuck doing the "do" of their business. They are the ones hands-on with production, perpetually involved in every minute detail. They rarely move into a position where they can truly scale their operations. Scaling, fundamentally, means ensuring you have excellent systems and processes in place.

I've seen this firsthand. Even the gentleman whose business I recently acquired, while incredibly successful, expressed a wish that he had approached things differently years ago. He was a great business owner, but he wasn't a builder in the truest sense until much later. My own parents, from whom I inherited my entrepreneurial spirit, owned their own company for as long as I can remember. They grew it well, but they, too, hit a capacity limit because they remained deeply entrenched in the daily operations.

The difference between a successful business owner and a true builder lies in the ability to abstract oneself from the direct execution. If you are stuck being the person who does the thing, you're the "horse" pulling the cart. There's just so much you can put in that cart before you can't move forward anymore. This is a common pitfall for small business owners. They are hesitant to hire employees, feeling that it is easier and less expensive to do everything oneself. What they don't realize is that this very mindset prevents them from breaking free and scaling.

Becoming the Engineer, Not Just the Horse

I hired my first assistant more than two decades ago, and I've been delegating ever since. To be honest, I no longer know how to do some of the things I used to do, and I shouldn't. It's not a productive use of my time. As a business owner, you must continuously assess how you allocate your time. Consider the example of a clothes store owner, such as your mother. If a woman designs the clothes, sets up the store, and opens and closes the store herself, she is the horse. While this is sometimes necessary for survival, particularly when first starting out, it eventually becomes a barrier to growth.

The goal is to figure out what you are actually uniquely good at. If she excels at creating garments, she should focus on bespoke pieces for high-value clients. Imagine her designing a dress and naming it after her favorite client, "The Michelle," in the same way that Hermes called the "Kelly" pocketbook after Grace Kelly. When you discover what you are really, really good at, that is ultimately the only thing you should be doing. That is how you build your company better.

This is the essence of becoming a builder: understanding how to delegate lower-value tasks to individuals who will grow into those positions and then using your freed-up time to engage in activities that truly drive your business forward. It is about developing the engine that will pull the train more efficiently and effectively, allowing it to carry more. You are no longer doing the heavy lifting; you are creating the system that does it for you. This allows for continuous growth, innovation, and, ultimately, the creation of a much larger, more valuable enterprise.

From Success to Legacy: The Builder's Mark

Many builders' ultimate goal is not only to achieve financial success in the short term but also to leave a lasting legacy. While Elon Musk's legacy is still being formed, his plan to colonize Mars is undeniably ambitious. Builders are not satisfied with simply earning wealth; they want their impact to last beyond their lifetime.

However, as I mentioned, many business owners, even successful ones, sell their businesses too late in life to embark on another significant building project. They achieve financial success but perhaps not the capacity to create multiple ventures or a self-sustaining empire. The difference lies in whether they were able to build their business to a point where it could operate without their constant, direct involvement.

The true builder cultivates the vision to take a step back, construct solid procedures, and empower a team to handle day-to-day tasks. This enables people to apply their unique skills to higher-level strategic thinking, creativity, and the identification of new opportunities. They evolve from vital operators to visionary leaders capable of replicating their success in several companies.

This is the journey of the builder: a relentless pursuit of creation fueled by a deep understanding of finance, taxation, business structures, and, most importantly, the power of systems and delegation. They are the rare individuals who truly shape the world around them, not just by accumulating assets but by building and expanding the very engines of wealth and innovation. While not everyone needs to be a builder, everyone can learn from their example – the importance of strategic thinking, the value of robust systems, and the courage to take calculated risks in pursuit of a grander vision. Their stories remind us that true wealth isn't just about what you have but what you build.

Chapter Eight: Money And Mindset: Breaking Barriers

Breaking through personal barriers starts with understanding the unique significance that money holds for each individual. Money is not merely currency; it symbolizes different things based on a person's life circumstances and mindset. For some, it represents survival—ensuring there is enough to cover basic needs like food, shelter, and safety. For others, money signifies the ability to indulge in comforts, save for the future, or build wealth and leave a legacy. This personal relationship with money is shaped by one's experiences, family background, and social environment.

To illustrate this point, let me share a personal experience. When I first started my business, my wife expressed that she would be happy when I reached an annual income of $100,000. I thought that was a reasonable goal. However, after achieving that milestone, the goalpost shifted to $150,000. I kept pushing myself and eventually surpassed $250,000. At that point, my wife realized that I wasn't going to stop chasing more. This experience taught me an important lesson: it's essential to be content and grateful for your current situation, but that doesn't mean you shouldn't strive for growth and improvement.

This mindset is crucial—it distinguishes between settling for less and truly thriving. Some may perceive constant striving as a sign of dissatisfaction or greed. For me, it's a reflection of my desire to continually improve, build a better life, and unlock new possibilities.

Another important distinction to make is regarding the phrase often misquoted as "Money is the root of all evil." The correct expression is "The love of money is the root of all evil." This subtle difference carries significant weight. Loving money purely for its own sake can lead to harmful behaviors—greed, selfishness, and unethical decisions. However, appreciating what money can do for you—providing freedom, security, and opportunities—is a healthy and motivating mindset.

Shifting your perspective from "I want more money because I love money" to "I want more money because it will help me live better, support my family, and create safety" transforms everything. It changes money from a source of anxiety or shame into a tool for empowerment.

Ultimately, understanding your personal barriers surrounding money begins with reflecting on what money means to you. Recognize that your relationship with money is deeply personal and shaped by your past experiences. Embrace a mindset that honors both gratitude for your current position and the ambition to grow, using money as a means to achieve freedom and security rather than an end in itself.

1. Visualizing and Setting Financial Goals

Breaking through barriers often begins with a shift in mindset—from simply surviving to striving for security and eventually, abundance. When you find yourself in survival mode, your focus is primarily on meeting basic needs: ensuring you have enough food, a roof over your head, and just getting through each day. It's a stressful existence, and financial goals can feel distant or even unattainable. However, transformation begins when you allow yourself to envision a different reality.

Visualizing yourself not only as a spender but as a saver and builder is a powerful catalyst for change. Instead of concentrating solely on immediate gratification or merely making ends meet, picture yourself setting money aside, investing in your future, and creating opportunities for growth. This mental shift opens doors to new behaviors and choices that align with the goal of building long-term financial stability.

Articulating these visions by sharing your goals with others can be immensely beneficial. Whether it's friends, family, mentors, or coaches, vocalizing your ambitions increases your accountability. When you say to someone, "This is what I'm working toward," you are not only making a commitment to yourself but also inviting support, feedback, and encouragement from your community.

Sharing your goals can ignite conversations that lead to new insights and information—perhaps ideas you hadn't previously considered, resources, or connections that help clarify your path. It also solidifies your goals, transforming them from abstract wishes into tangible targets that you actively pursue.

2. The Power of Sharing Goals and Accountability

One of the most effective strategies for breaking through barriers is to openly share your goals. When you announce your ambitions publicly—whether to friends, family, or mentors—you ignite a powerful process. This act not only holds you accountable but also invites new perspectives, insights, and opportunities that you might not have discovered on your own.

Sharing your goals often leads to meaningful conversations. People may offer advice, share resources, or provide encouragement that fuels your momentum. As you verbalize your vision and receive feedback, you gain clarity that helps refine your approach. This network of support becomes an invaluable asset in your journey toward growth.

However, be prepared for some resistance. Not everyone will react positively to your ambitions. Doubt, skepticism, or even negativity can arise, sometimes from those closest to you. Comments like "That's unrealistic," or "You're dreaming too big," can serve as barriers in themselves. When this occurs, it's a crucial opportunity to evaluate the influence of the people around you.

Your environment and relationships have a significant impact on your mindset and progress. Surround yourself with individuals who energize and inspire you—those who genuinely support your growth and believe in your potential. Conversely, consider distancing yourself emotionally or physically from those who drain your energy or undermine your confidence.

3. The Importance of Your Social Environment

Your social environment plays a crucial role in either fueling your growth or holding you back. A powerful way to assess your relationships is by categorizing the people in your life into two groups: those who fill your bucket and those who drain it. Bucket fillers are the individuals who energize you, inspire you, and genuinely support your goals. They celebrate your progress and challenge you to grow. In contrast, bucket drainers consistently sap your energy, bring negativity, and can hinder your personal development.

Navigating relationships—especially with family—can be complex. Family members who drain your energy often do so unintentionally, creating emotional obstacles that can be difficult to manage. While it's important to be there for family during times of need, it's equally vital to set boundaries that protect your mental and emotional well-being. Growth requires space, and sometimes that means limiting contact with those who consistently pull you down.

To effectively break through barriers, you must surround yourself with people who challenge you intellectually, emotionally, and professionally. Being around individuals who inspire you to push beyond your limits cultivates an environment conducive to growth. It's essential to find spaces—whether physical or virtual—where you are not the most knowledgeable person. When you're always the smartest in the room, it's easy to fall into stagnation and complacency.

Growth flourishes in environments characterized by collaboration, challenge, and shared learning. Seek out mentors, peers, and communities that elevate your thinking and broaden your horizons. Remember, breaking barriers is not solely about internal mindset shifts; it also involves the external influences you allow into your life.

4. Authenticity Over Appearance

In today's world, it's all too easy to get swept up in the "fake it till you make it" culture. Many individuals project an image of success by leasing luxury cars, renting upscale apartments, or showcasing designer clothes—often masking financial struggles behind this facade. It's essential to be discerning about who you choose to model your goals after, prioritizing authenticity over appearance.

A personal example illustrates this point effectively: Before the 2008 housing crisis, while many friends used their home equity to remodel and create stunning living spaces, my wife and I opted for a different approach. Instead of upgrading our kitchen, we invested in rental properties that built long-term equity and financial stability. Although our home may not have appeared as impressive, our balance sheet told a very different story—one of patient wealth-building rather than superficial spending.

Social media often exacerbates this issue by presenting only highlight reels—the vacations, new cars, and luxurious moments—while obscuring the everyday struggles, sacrifices, and hard work that occur behind the scenes. People frequently compare their real lives to these curated snapshots, leading to unrealistic expectations and unnecessary pressure.

5. Patience and Long-Term Perspective

True success rarely happens overnight. It requires time, consistent effort, and steady progress to transition from where you are today to where you aspire to be tomorrow. Recognizing this reality helps maintain motivation and alleviates the frustration that often accompanies slow progress.

A crucial aspect of this journey is shifting your mindset to align with the future you desire. Visualizing yourself already living in that improved reality prepares your mind to take the necessary actions and remain resilient in the face of challenges.

I once set a goal to earn $1 million in a single year—a milestone that took me 20 years to achieve. When I finally reached it, I was surprised by the emptiness I felt afterward. Having pursued that target for so long, I suddenly found myself asking, "What's next?" This moment of reflection led to a deeper understanding: goals are not just destinations but stepping stones toward ongoing growth and purpose.

6. Continuous Learning and Resilience

Breaking through barriers is rarely a straightforward journey. It often involves setbacks, losses, and moments of doubt. The key to growth lies in looking inward when faced with challenges—asking yourself what you can learn and how you can improve. This mindset transforms failures into valuable lessons rather than reasons to give up.

Maintaining a positive outlook, even when things don't go your way, is essential. For instance, when a client departs or a deal falls through, instead of fixating on the loss, view it as an opportunity to forge new and better connections. Life will inevitably knock you down; resilience is about getting back up, adapting, and moving forward without repeating the same mistakes.

Remember, mistakes don't define your progress—repeated mistakes do. To continue leveling up, you must commit to continuous learning, self-reflection, and personal growth. Surround yourself with individuals who inspire you, seek knowledge from books, mentors, and experiences, and remain open to evolving your strategies as you advance. Embrace the journey of resilience, knowing that each challenge is an opportunity for growth and development.

Maslow's Hierarchy of Needs

The strategies outlined in this chapter align closely with Abraham Maslow's Hierarchy of Needs, a psychological framework that explains human motivation as a progression through five levels of needs. These levels—physiological, safety, love and belonging, esteem, and self-actualization—are often depicted as a pyramid, with each level building upon the one below.

Physiological Needs and Safety

Breaking barriers begins with addressing foundational needs, such as financial security and basic survival. This includes having enough money for essentials like food, shelter, and peace of mind. These needs form the base of Maslow's hierarchy and must be met before individuals can focus on higher levels of growth.

- **Love and Belonging:** Sharing your goals, setting boundaries, and fostering supportive relationships fulfill the social need for connection and acceptance. These actions align with Maslow's third level, which emphasizes the importance of meaningful relationships and a sense of belonging.
- **Esteem:** Surrounding yourself with inspiring individuals, committing to continuous learning, and achieving personal milestones build confidence and self-respect. These efforts correspond to Maslow's esteem level, which focuses on gaining recognition, respect, and a sense of accomplishment.
- **Self-Actualization:** Setting ambitious goals, reflecting on your purpose, and committing to lifelong growth drive you

toward self-actualization—the pinnacle of Maslow's hierarchy. This stage represents the fulfillment of your potential and the pursuit of personal meaning and purpose.

Much like Maslow's model, the strategies in this chapter emphasize starting with foundational needs—securing safety and stability—before progressing to higher levels of growth. For example:

- **Mindset and Goal-Setting:** These strategies help you move from survival to security and eventually to abundance, mirroring the progression through Maslow's hierarchy.
- **Accountability and Social Environment:** Building supportive relationships and sharing your goals align with the need for love, belonging, and esteem.
- **Authenticity, Patience, and Resilience:** These qualities foster self-respect and long-term growth, paving the way for self-actualization.

By addressing each level thoughtfully, you create a sustainable path for breaking barriers and achieving meaningful success. Just as Maslow's hierarchy suggests, meeting needs progressively allows you to unlock your full potential and live a more fulfilled life.

By understanding how these needs interconnect, it becomes clear that breaking financial and personal barriers is not solely about money; it's about fulfilling fundamental human drives step by step.

For instance, when you transition from merely surviving financially to feeling secure, you are addressing the physiological and safety levels of Maslow's pyramid. Establishing boundaries with negative influences and cultivating positive relationships satisfies your social needs, creating a supportive environment in which you can thrive.

As you set and share your goals, push past doubts, and surround yourself with those who challenge and inspire you, you build esteem—both from within and from others. This boost in confidence serves as a catalyst for further growth.

Conclusion

The strategies discussed in this chapter—from mindset shifts and goal visualization to managing relationships and cultivating resilience—align seamlessly with Maslow's hierarchy. They guide you through the process of first meeting your foundational needs and then empowering you to grow socially, emotionally, and intellectually.

As Maslow taught, true transformation occurs when you progress through these levels deliberately and mindfully. This chapter lays the groundwork for the rest of the book, which will continue to explore how to apply these principles in practical ways, helping you break barriers and reach your full potential at every stage of your journey.

Chapter Nine: Money With Purpose – Redefining Success

Money as a Tool, Not the Goal

When you're in a survival mindset, it's easy to feel that money is the only thing that matters. Every decision revolves around securing enough funds to cover essentials like rent, groceries, or unexpected repairs. This is completely understandable. In those moments, money can seem like the ultimate objective—the destination, the prize. However, it's crucial to reframe our perspective on money. Ultimately, money should not be seen as the goal; rather, it is a tool that helps you achieve your goals.

This shift in mindset can be incredibly empowering. Instead of fixating on a specific sum in your bank account, you can focus on using that money to create the life you desire. This may involve achieving financial security, enjoying the freedom to travel, supporting your family, or even having the confidence to embark on new ventures. The essence of money lies not in merely accumulating it, but in utilizing it to serve your higher purpose.

However, there's a caveat: when you're merely trying to survive, it's tough to adopt this mindset. The immediate need to make ends meet often overshadows any long-term aspirations. In these times, you might not be dreaming about legacy or purpose; you're just focused on getting through the week. And that's perfectly okay. The first step is recognizing your current situation. Once you find a bit of breathing room, remember this: money works best as a servant to your goals, not as your master.

A significant aspect of this equation is the way you earn your money. If you're stuck in a job you despise, earning money can feel like a heavy burden. Each dollar earned might feel like it's come at the expense of your well-being. Conversely, if you find joy or meaning in your work—even if the pay isn't ideal—earning can become lighter and more fulfilling. When you enjoy the way you make your money, you tend to treat it with greater respect. It transforms from just a paycheck into a vital part of your journey toward a life that feels aligned with your values.

So, if you're feeling trapped or exhausted by your current earning situation, consider asking yourself: Is there a path toward something more fulfilling, even if it's just a small step? Money earned with passion and intention holds a different kind of power—it not only supports your financial needs but also fuels your sense of purpose.

Getting Out of Survival Mode

Survival mode can often feel like being trapped in quicksand—you're doing everything possible just to stay afloat. Even when you sense that change is necessary, fear tends to keep you anchored. This fear can manifest as anxiety over failure, dread of the unknown, or reluctance to leave behind the small sense of security you have. Most significantly, it often revolves around a fear of change.

A major reason people remain stuck in survival mode is the overwhelming fear of making a move. Perhaps you're in a job that no longer fulfills you—or maybe it never did—but the thought of putting yourself out there can feel paralyzing. Job interviews, new environments, and different responsibilities all seem like huge risks when you're already feeling drained. It's completely natural to feel this way.

However, here's a truth that may be uncomfortable to accept: to create a better life, you must navigate through that discomfort. You have to take the interview. You need to send out that resume. You must confront rejection and rise again. No one enjoys hearing "no," but remember that with each rejection, you're one step closer to the right "yes."

Growth cannot occur in comfort. The longer you avoid change, the longer you remain stagnant. Yet, once you start taking those initial steps—no matter how small—the momentum begins to build. The discomfort may not vanish, but your confidence will grow. Suddenly, what once seemed impossible becomes manageable. You'll discover that you can handle more than you initially believed. You'll evolve beyond your previous self.

I've witnessed this transformation repeatedly. Those who embrace discomfort and confront challenges head-on are the ones who progress—not always swiftly or smoothly, but they move forward nonetheless.

So, if you find yourself feeling stuck, remember this: you're not broken, nor are you lazy. You're simply grappling with fear—and that's perfectly okay. Don't allow fear to take the reins. Let it sit in the backseat while you take control of the wheel. Because the sooner you choose to act despite your fears, the sooner you'll find that life begins to unfold in new and exciting ways.

Practical Examples from the Financial Industry

In the financial sector, a clear and consistent pattern emerges: technical brilliance alone is insufficient. You might be the most skilled analyst, adept at dissecting complex investment strategies, interpreting market patterns with finesse, and accurately assessing risk. However, if you can't engage effectively with people, you risk remaining invisible.

Many of the brightest finance professionals I've encountered struggle with client interactions. It's not that they lack care or concern; rather, the thought of sitting face-to-face with a client, explaining insights, answering questions, and building trust can be daunting. They often retreat to the numbers, hoping that their results will speak for themselves. But the reality is that, in this industry—and indeed in life—people seek more than just results; they crave connection.

Success often hinges on your ability to put yourself out there. The advisors who flourish, who cultivate robust client bases and expand their practices, are typically those who excel at both technical and relational skills. They don't just manage money effectively; they also know how to communicate value, listen to concerns, and build trust.

Simply being willing to show up, make eye contact, and say, "Here's how I can help you," can make a significant difference. Like any other skill, this can be learned. I've worked with professionals who initially felt anxious about public speaking or were nervous in one-on-

one client interactions. Over time, with practice, they not only improved but began to enjoy it. Confidence stems from action, not just thought.

I've even begun teaching these principles to my daughters. I remember my own fear of presenting in front of a classroom when I was younger, so I made it a point to help my kids develop these skills early on. Now, they volunteer to present during group projects, and while their classmates may breathe a sigh of relief, they step up and deliver. They've learned that speaking up isn't about being the smartest in the room—it's about the willingness to show up.

One of the most fulfilling experiences I've had as a parent is sharing lessons I learned the hard way—particularly those surrounding confidence and communication.

As a child, I was absolutely petrified of public speaking. I can vividly recall the anxiety that washed over me whenever a teacher announced group presentations. I would sit there, silently praying not to be chosen, dreading the moment I'd have to stand in front of my classmates. My voice would tremble, my thoughts would scatter, and all I wanted was to disappear. It wasn't until I was much older—well into my professional life—that I finally confronted that fear through extensive training and practice.

Recognizing how valuable this skill became for me, I made it a priority to start early with my daughters. I wanted to spare them from experiencing the same fear in adulthood. So, I began teaching them how to present, speak clearly, and lead a room—even if it was just their classroom. We started with the basics: rehearsing school projects, structuring their talks, and encouraging them to take the lead during group activities.

And it paid off! Today, both of my daughters are the first to raise their hands when a group presentation opportunity arises. While other students hope to avoid speaking, my girls confidently step up. They even took this newfound skill to a whole new level—they once created a detailed PowerPoint presentation to negotiate their Christmas and birthday gift lists with their mom and me. It was well-researched, visually appealing, and delivered with an assurance that genuinely surprised me. I had to respect their hustle!

What's fascinating is how this confidence extends beyond schoolwork or family negotiations; it's also preparing them for real life. The ability to communicate effectively, advocate for themselves, or simply stand tall in a room filled with people is a skill that yields benefits in any field. Whether it's interviewing for a job, leading a project, or negotiating a salary, it all begins with the ability to speak up for oneself.

Moving into "Spender Mode"

After successfully navigating your way out of pure survival mode, you may find yourself entering what I refer to as "spender mode." This is the stage where you have a bit more breathing room. You're no longer just scraping by; instead, you have enough space to think about things beyond the next bill. In this phase, how you present yourself to the world becomes increasingly important.

I'm not discussing vanity here—I'm talking about self-investment. Perhaps you decide to spend a little extra on your wardrobe to feel more confident in your own skin. That boost in self-image can translate into greater confidence during job interviews, networking events, or even when asserting yourself in your current role.

This is the moment to get strategic. Ask yourself: Is your current job maximizing your skills, time, and value? If the answer is no, it's time to start preparing for your next move. This might involve pursuing a promotion, applying for a new position, or seeking additional training to enhance your qualifications. You need to take steps toward the version of your life you aspire to live—even if those steps are small and incremental at first.

However, here's the hard truth: you can't always fix a toxic environment. Sometimes, despite your efforts to improve your surroundings, the workplace culture remains detrimental, or your manager may be so limiting that it stifles your growth. In such cases, the best course of action may be to walk away and seek a new opportunity where your talents are valued and nurtured.

No matter how uncomfortable it may feel, change is often the gateway to growth. Remaining in a situation that drains you simply because it's familiar leads to a slow erosion of your potential. You deserve better, and sometimes that means having the belief in yourself to go out and find it.

The Legacy Dilemma

This is a conversation I frequently have with clients—especially those who are approaching or already in retirement. There's a deeply rooted desire to leave something behind for the next generation. It's a noble intention that stems from love, but too often, it can transform into a burden.

I've encountered clients who have saved just enough to retire comfortably, yet they find themselves more anxious about leaving money for their children than securing their own peace of mind.

That's where I come in—not to dismiss their concerns, but to help reframe them.

Unless your children face unique circumstances, such as special needs or permanent dependency, your primary responsibility is to yourself. You've dedicated a lifetime to work, and you've earned the right to enjoy your retirement. Don't downsize your dreams or limit your lifestyle simply to increase an inheritance that your children may not even need or appreciate in the way you envision.

I often remind my clients with this phrase: "Your kids can inherit what's left—but don't live your life as if they come first now that they're grown." You've raised them, educated them, and instilled values and tools for their success. Now it's your time to thrive. There's wisdom in living well, not just in planning to give well.

Wealth and Generational Planning

As clients build their wealth, the conversation naturally shifts toward legacy—not just what they leave behind, but how they leave it. For many, it's no longer solely about having enough; it's about creating a lasting impact across generations.

A common phrase I hear is, "Charity begins at home." For these clients, this means providing meaningful support to their children and grandchildren—whether that's helping with a down payment on a home, funding a reliable car, or contributing to college tuition. These gifts can significantly enhance someone's trajectory when given at the right time.

However, equally important—perhaps even more so—is the need to teach financial responsibility alongside that support.

In my own life, I witness this principle in action. My older daughter has been managing her own debit card since she was 13. She has displayed remarkable responsibility, budgeting her spending and tracking her balances. In contrast, my younger daughter, now also 13, chose to decline the offer of a debit card. Her reasoning? "I don't trust myself yet." This kind of self-awareness at a young age is powerful; it demonstrates maturity and an understanding that managing money involves readiness, not just access.

Both approaches are valid. One daughter is eager to engage, while the other is wisely cautious. What matters most is nurturing the values and environment where both decisions are respected and encouraged.

Children Are Individuals

Regardless of whether your children are adopted or biological, one undeniable truth remains: no two are the same. Even when raised in the same household, with identical values, routines, and opportunities, each child develops their own unique personality, instincts, and relationship with money.

Understanding this individuality is crucial when teaching financial literacy and planning a legacy. A one-size-fits-all approach simply doesn't work.

Some children are natural savers—cautious, analytical, and deliberate with every dollar. Others may be more spontaneous, generous to a fault, or motivated by experiences rather than security. Neither approach is inherently wrong, but each requires a tailored method of guidance.

In my own family, this has become very evident. Despite being raised together, my daughters display completely different money personalities. One is assertive, confident, and financially proactive—eager to take control of her finances. The other is introspective, self-aware, and possesses a strong sense of when she's ready for more responsibility.

Recognizing these differences has taught me that effective parenting—and successful legacy building—requires adapting to each child's temperament. This could mean granting one more freedom while providing the other with more structure. It may also involve revisiting discussions about money at different times, based on their emotional and cognitive readiness.

Tools for Legacy Building

Modern financial tools, such as Donor-Advised Funds (DAFs), offer effective strategies for building and preserving your legacy while minimizing tax burdens. These instruments are particularly valuable for families with substantial retirement assets.

For instance, large Individual Retirement Accounts (IRAs) can generate significant tax liabilities for heirs. When inherited, these accounts often require mandatory withdrawals within a decade, which can push beneficiaries into higher tax brackets, ultimately reducing the overall inheritance.

By directing an IRA into a Donor-Advised Fund upon death, you can avoid these immediate tax consequences. The fund then distributes income to your children over their lifetimes, potentially spanning 30 to 40 years or more, depending on their ages. This extended timeline helps preserve more wealth and offers a steadier source of income.

Ultimately, when your children pass, any remaining assets in the fund can be transferred to your chosen charities. This approach creates a triple benefit: it reduces taxes, provides long-term support for your heirs, and ensures a lasting charitable impact.

While not all financial advisors are familiar with these tools, they represent powerful options for those looking to make their money work smarter for their families and the causes they care about.

Appendix

Next Steps: Practical Guidance for Your Financial Journey

Whether you're just beginning your financial journey or refining an established plan, here are some actionable next steps to help you continue building toward your legacy:

- **If you're in debt:**
    - Connect with a certified debt counselor to develop a sustainable payoff plan.
    - Prioritize high-interest debt and consolidate if it makes sense for your situation.
- **If you're ready to start saving:**
    - Open a high-yield savings account or a Roth IRA.
    - Set up automated transfers for consistent contributions.
- **If you want to invest:**
    - Work with a fiduciary financial advisor who understands your money mindset and values.

- Focus on long-term strategies over short-term gains.

➢ **If you're navigating financial conversations:**

- Schedule family meetings to discuss shared goals and expectations.
- Practice open, value-based conversations around money.

➢ **If you're building your financial literacy:**

- Read trustworthy books, attend workshops, or listen to personal finance podcasts.
- Stay curious—your financial mindset will grow as your knowledge does

Epilogue

Your Story, Your Legacy

This book began with the premise that wealth isn't just about dollars and cents—it's about meaning, mindset, and mission. Throughout the pages, you've explored how to make intentional choices that reflect your values and build a life of purpose and security.

Whether you're just starting out or you've been on this path for years, know that financial empowerment is a journey, not a destination. There will be progress and setbacks, clarity and confusion—but through it all, the mindset you bring to money will shape not only your life, but the lives of those who follow you.

You now have the tools to build a legacy—not just of wealth, but of wisdom. And in doing so, you're not just changing your own life. You're expanding what's possible for others.

Stay intentional. Stay resilient. And above all, stay rooted in your "why."

What's Next?

Are Retirement Accounts Really Good for You... Or Just for the Government?

From the upcoming book by Julie

Most of us have been told that saving into retirement accounts is a smart financial move. And while that's often true, is it the *whole* truth?

In my next book, we'll dive into the real long-term implications of tax-deferred accounts like 401(k)s and traditional IRAs. What's the true cost of deferring taxes now, only to face much higher tax bills later?

Here's a preview:

"As a 30-year-old, deferring $1,000 into a retirement account might save you $150 in taxes today. But by the time you're 60 or 70, that $1,000 could have grown to $40,000 or more—and you might owe $14,000 or more in taxes on it. Was that original $150 savings really worth it?"

We'll explore:

- The tax trade-offs of traditional retirement plans
- The opportunity costs of locking your money away
- Smarter ways to grow wealth with flexibility and control
- How to align your retirement strategy with your overall legacy plan

This next book will challenge conventional wisdom and offer modern strategies to help you make retirement planning work for you—not just the government.

www.ingramcontent.com/pod-product-compliance
Lightning Source LLC
LaVergne TN
LVHW011519200926
848484LV00001B/74